AN ISLAND IN THE SKY

Selected Poetry of Al Pittman

EDITED BY MARTIN WARE AND STEPHANIE MCKENZIE

An Island in the Sky

Selected Poetry of Al Pittman

EDITED BY MARTIN WARE AND STEPHANIE MCKENZIE

BREAKWATER BOOKS

BREAKWATER

P.O. Box 2188, 100 Water Street, St. John's, NL, A1C 6E6
www.breakwaterbooks.com

National Library of Canada Cataloguing in Publication
Pittman, Al, 1940-2001
An Island in the Sky : Selected Poetry of Al Pittman /
Martin Ware and Stephanie Mckenzie, editors.
Includes bibliographical references.
ISBN 1-55081-199-1
I. Ware, Martin II. McKenzie, Stephanie III. Title.
PS8531.I86I84 2003   C811'.54   C2003-902322-2
PR9199.3.P52J84 2003

© 2003 Estate of Al Pittman
Cover/Design/Layout: Rhonda Molloy

ALL RIGHTS RESERVED. No part of this work covered by the copyright hereon may be reproduced or used in any form or by any means—graphic, electronic or mechanical—without the prior written permission of the publisher. Any request for photocopying, recording, taping or storing in an information retrieval system of any part of this book shall be directed in writing to the Canadian Reprography Collective, 6 Adelaide Street East, Suite 900, Toronto, Ontario, M5C 1H6. This applies to classroom usage as well.

We acknowledge the financial support of The Canada Council for the Arts
for our publishing activities.

 We acknowledge the financial support of the Government of Canada through the Book Publishing Industry Development Program (BPIDP) for our publishing activities.

Printed in Canada.

Then one day
in the warmth of the sun
we undressed and tip-toed
into the swirling foam
at the pool's edge
and holding on to each other's hands
we waded laughing
into one more summer.

—Len Margaret,
"One More Summer"

Acknowledgements

Many people helped make this publication possible.

We would like to thank Molly Ware, Barbara Rose, John Steffler, Marilee Pittman, Kyran Pittman, Emily Pittman, Clyde Rose, Rex Brown, Adrian Fowler, Marc Thackray, Wilfred Wareham, Anita Best, Pat Byrne, Randy Maggs, Rosalie Elliott, Pauline Hayes, Pam Parsons, and Arlene Buckle.

—Martin Ware & Stephanie McKenzie

Contents

Introduction 13
Discovering Al Pittman's Poems 32
Textual Note 34

From *The Elusive Resurrection* (1966)

The Berry Pickers 38
The Border 39
Baptism 40

From *Seaweed and Rosaries* (1968)

St. Leonard's Revisited 42
The Cost of a Good Canoe .43
Going to Get Water 45
Boys at Baseball 47
Guilty as Charged 49
Searston Beach 50
Angels 51
Homecoming 52

From *Through One More Window* (1974)

Cooks Brook 54
Big City Skyline 56
The Echo of the Ax 57
Celebration 58
St. Joseph's Feastday, Fogo Island 60
Her Portrait of Me 61
Poem for Marilee Sleeping 62
Island Estate at St. Andrew's 64
Gram Glover's Dream 66
On the Road to LaScie 68
Faith Healer 70
Prose Poems 72
Brimstone Head 77
Shanadithit 79

From *Once When I Was Drowning* (1977)

Lines for My Grandfather Long Gone 84
Poem for a Young Man
Who Froze to Death Down North, Nov. '77. 87
I Leave My Prayers 89
Old Soldiers 90
Driftwood 92
Song Also 93
Confession 94
Winter '72 95
The Pigeon on the Gate 96
One Night in Winnipeg 97
Declaration of War 99
Funeral 101
April 103
Angelmaker 104

From *Dancing in Limbo* (1993)

Atlantis 106
Goodnight Kiss 107
Grace before Meals 109
Boxing the Compass 110
Passing through St. Jude's 113
Charmer 116
What My Father Said about Sound 119
Maiden Voyage 121
Father of the Bride 123
The Cat in the Snow 125
The Voices Downstairs 127
The Woman in the Waterfront Bar 129
The Dandelion Killers 131
The Agony in the Garden 133
Ashes, Ashes! All Fall Down! 135
Prayer 139
Kelly at Graveside 141
The Dance of the Mayflies 143
Limbo Dancer 144

FROM *Thirty-for-Sixty* (2000)

The Pink, White and Green 148
Lupins 150
The Citrus Sea 152
Lambs to the Slaughter .154
Standing Room Only 156
Hard Times 159
Another Night in Crawley's Cove 160
The Sea Breeze Lounge .162
The Fuller Brush Man 164
Thirty-for-Sixty 166
A River Runs through Her 168
A Bouquet for Emily 170
The Annunciation 172
To Kyran in Full Flight .173
Homecoming 176
Rites of Passage 178

Introduction

EACH PERSON WHO knew Al Pittman well will be able to conjure up a favourite image of him. The image may be of him holding one of his small grandsons. It may be of him standing, reading his poetry "with the voice of a rusty nail," holding his book in one hand, and beating out the poem's measure with his other.[1] Or it may be of him sitting at his corner bar stool at Casual Jack's, rapt in conversation with an old friend or a complete stranger, while squeezing a typescript which a young writer had slipped onto the counter. Then again, it may be of Al sitting at his special window seat in Clyde Rose's house at Crawley's Cove, a glass of screech in his hand, looking over the rounded Bonne Bay hills and listening to his friends singing a rousing ballad.

Many of these images remind one of how important Al's family, friends and poetry were in his life. Some of the images may also suggest his unusual capacity for creating fellow feeling and the endless pleasure he took in listening and conversing. The respect that he had for ordinary people and their unique experiences is reflected in his idea of the poet. He thought that to aspire to be a poet was to aspire to a role which was the treasure of the world, that the poet's influence was vital to the life of a healthy community, and that it was natural for people to honour and enjoy poetry and song. These ideas are reflected in the enormous energy he devoted to revising and shaping his poems so they would sound and read well and give heightened expression to what anybody might experience. He wanted people to read, hear and take delight in poetry. He was in a great many ways a people's poet.

The purpose of this collection is to broadly represent Al's lifetime work in poetry and make it available to as wide a circle of readers as possible. It is neither definitive nor, in any way, the last word. In the final year of his life, Al was under the power of a great surge of imaginative energy. He was writing poems (for a projected book), working on a new dramatic piece (*The Moon Also Rises*), and much involved in the efforts which led to a Newfoundland company touring his play *West Moon* in Ireland during the late fall of 2001.[2] All the while, he was constantly caught up in working with his group of young creative writers, encouraging, inspiring, provoking, challenging, scrutinizing and criticizing them, and taking part in their public readings. It certainly seemed as if he had wonderful work still to do.

Then came the overwhelming and numbing fact of his death in late August, 2001. Just about everyone who had the slightest acquaintance with Al knew how ill and frail he was, but, to many, it seemed inconceivable that such a vital person could be taken away. The widespread outpouring of grief and the several evenings, readings and concerts devoted to his memory reflected not only a general and deeply felt sense of loss but also a resolve to keep his memory alive.[3] He wrote in a prose poem of his difficulty in writing poems for dead friends, and in it suggested that to do so would be like "chipping in with skilled precision the last digit on your own gravestone."[4] However, this is not the time to chip out any niche for Al. Though he is absent in body, he seems very much present in spirit, especially in the minds of those who love his poetry and songs, and these will have the decisive influence in determining the parts of his work which eventually will live.

What Stephanie McKenzie and I have tried to do in editing this collection is to bring together those poems which particularly reflect the poetry of Al Pittman over four decades and six volumes of writing. We have deliberately omitted his most recent poetry, both because it is still scattered and because it may provide the basis for a short new volume.

What follows is by way of being an invitation as much as an introduction—an invitation to explore the bittersweet, intensely human, beautifully crafted and sometimes enigmatic poems of Al Pittman. It is an invitation to take up this book in much the same spirit as you would step out to one of those remarkable March Hare evenings in Corner Brook, the annual weekends of poetry and music which have so much in common with a traditional Newfoundland "time." This is the moment to anticipate the many moods and twists of Al's poetry, to attune your ear to his voice in all its variety: tender, reminiscent, lyrical, teasing, often ironic, sometimes bemused, occasionally agonizing and filled with alarm, exploring "the ruined regions of the heart."[5]

It was Al's voice which especially appealed to fellow Newfoundlander Carl Leggo, who has written "you were the first poet / whose voice in my ear / was not alien."[6] For those who have heard Al read, his voice will still ring in the ears "gruff and rough and sweet." But he did not find his voice easily. He has written, "I was in my early twenties before I started to write out of my own mind, voice and out of imagery with which I was totally familiar. There finally came a time when I was not trying to duplicate somebody else's work, and that was when I really began."[7] This discovery was important for his fellow Newfoundland poets. Until the mid nineteen sixties, when Al discovered his poetic style, Newfoundland poetry, for most Canadians, was synonymous with the heroic poetry of E. J. Pratt. Pratt frequently depicts "the mighty clashes between man and the elements," and his imagery is full of "crags, sea gulls, icebergs, fog, men foundering in small boats, women waiting at open doors."[8] Pratt's work does not offer a familiar and homely world. Almost all of it is contained within a fairly strict metrical and rhyming strait jacket, which does not allow for the natural rhythms of the speaking voice. One of Al's great gifts, in common with other poets, has been to rediscover a simple, earthy, first-person voice, heightened on occasion and reflecting his own experience, as it was shaped by the everyday concerns, the love and longing, the fantasies and dreams, the darkness, the quirks, pangs and pains of the people of small-town and outport Newfoundland.

For Al, the reading and writing of poetry belong in places where ordinary people gather to share their friendships, to tell their stories, to enjoy themselves, to discover one another—places like Casual Jack's, the Columbus Club and the bars of the Glynmill Inn in Corner Brook, the packed rooms of the Ship Inn in St John's, the Sea Breeze Lounge or the wharf at Woody Point in Bonne Bay (where the men of the community once gathered after a day on the water to exchange jokes and cuffers). His is a poetry completely at home in lively back kitchens after midnight–a poetry closely associated with contemporary folk and ballad singers, and with the music of the fiddle, the accordion, the mouth organ and the tin whistle. It is a poetry which reflects the human landscape of modern Newfoundland alive with mischief, wrong-headedness and tenderness, where the traditional outport has been uprooted but not forgotten, and where people seek the old communal strength in honouring the generations and extended family, welcoming home the wanderers and discovering how much poets, artists and musicians have to learn from one another.

One of Al's forbears, Peter the Poet from St Leonard's, Placentia Bay, had composed songs which express comparable local themes.[9] Al has a good deal in common with this Peter (Peter Leonard) and the hundreds of community singers like him who enlivened pre-confederation Newfoundland. But in the practice of his craft, he is also up-to-date, being influenced by his dear friend, the New Brunswick poet Alden Nowlan; by fellow Newfoundlanders Tom Dawe and Enos Watts; and by kindred spirits like Dylan Thomas, e. e. cummings, Robert Frost, Paul Durcan and Archibald MacLeish. Their influence helped him to create a strongly contemporary note in his poetry. Yet several of the characteristics of the community singer of old Newfoundland remained strong in him. The community singer was usually the heart and soul of "the time" with its midnight lunch ("scoff"), its songs and ballads, its dancing, its recitations (for example, monologues) and dramatic entertainments.[10] Like the community singer, Al wrote ballads (a well-known one is "The Rocks of Merasheen") and loved a "time."[11] He has, however, greatly extended the scope of the Newfoundland imagination, taking recitations into a new dimension with plays for voices, like *Rope Against the Sun*, and utterly transforming and refining the art of the outport versifier.

Al's work as a poet encompasses a wide range of writing because virtually all of it is shaped by the poet's ear, the poet's sense of rhythm and the poet's precise imagery. This collection of his poetry only takes in a small part of his poetic work, if poetry is thus broadly defined. It does not include his poetic dramas, *Rope Against the Sun*, *West Moon* and *This Side of Heaven*, or the short stories of *The Boughwolfen*, or his books for children, *Down by Jim Long's Stage*, *On a Wing and a Wish* and *One Wonderful Fine Day for a Sculpin Named Sam*. It does not even include any of his ballads or lullabies, for that matter.

What the book does aim at is to give a selection of the best poems Al wrote over the last forty years so that the reader can linger over them, savour them and catch the nuances and shifts of perspective in a way that is not possible at an oral reading. This collection also provides the reader with a chance to enjoy Al's poems in context, to see how they gain strength from each other and to understand how they reflect a human and imaginative odyssey. In order to facilitate this, the poems have been arranged in rough chronological order, beginning with three pieces from his first book, *The Elusive Resurrection* (1966), and moving through selections from two youthful books, *Seaweed and Rosaries* (1968) and *Through One More Window* (1974). Then we come to a substantial representation from his most comprehensive selection, *Once When I was Drowning* (1978), a mid-career book. Finally, the book closes with selections from his two later books, *Dancing in Limbo* (1997) and *Thirty for Sixty* (2000), which round out and deepen Al's individual perspective.

What leaps out from a perusal of this collection as a whole is a recurring pattern of loss and rediscovery. Perhaps the origins of this pattern go back to the making of Al as a poet. He did not begin to write poetry until he was in his mid-twenties—that is, until he left Newfoundland to live in Montreal in 1964. This was a special time in Al's life, the time when he fell in love with his future wife, Marilee, and when he formed life-long friendships with Clyde Rose (later a well-known publisher) and with the singer and folklorist Pat Byrne, two members of the large Newfoundland community in Montreal.[12] He also joined the circle of writers associated with Ray Fraser and the little magazine *Intercourse* (of which he was to become editor). Al was always to remember the vitality of the Montreal years, especially the bars, places "packed tight / french, english, and italian curses blistering the blue air / [he] and [his] friends half stoned / on poetry and beer."[13] Often, though, he felt the strong pull of home.

Montreal could not offer him the imaginative sustenance he needed. He knew that he must return to Newfoundland, to the homes of his mother and father in Placentia Bay, "to put all the stories that they had ever told [him] in proper perspective."[14] So in the summer of 1967 with his new wife, Marilee, he travelled to the Island of Merasheen. More than anything else, this trip provided him with a poetic beginning, but there was also deep pain associated with it. His visit coincided with an ending, the last garden party held on the island, for this was the year of resettlement, the last year that the skippers of Merasheen—men like Anthony Wilson, George Wilson, Stan Ennis, Mike Casey—would fish out of the island's harbours. Like thousands of others around the Newfoundland coast, they were to suffer what amounted to involuntary eviction from their age-old communities and to be forced into growth centres and the alien rhythms of urban life. Al's essay "Death of an Outport" catches the immediacy of a death sentence on an entire way of life, and his experience that summer on Merasheen was to influence directly or indirectly everything that he was later to write.[15] Its immediate effect was to produce an outpouring of writing, and, surely, it was the catalyst for the strengthening of his poetic impulse.

The effect of the 1967 visit can best be understood by recognizing to what an extent outport consciousness was second nature to Al. While he had been born in the Placentia Bay community of St Leonard's, he had been taken away from it in his infancy, and he only made occasional visits to it as a small child. His childhood, adolescence and early manhood had all been spent in the West Coast paper-mill town of Corner Brook. He remembers that though he had not visited the island of Merasheen (his father's home) since he was four years old, he knew the community like "the palm of his hand." He says of his exploration of Merasheen:

> I had no guide, but I knew where every house was, used to be, whose hayfield was this, whose old fence was this, where the well was. I knew all this. I had never taken a note. I had no map with me. But I knew all this.[16]

Al's account reveals the Newfoundland bayman's special sense of home. His comments put a fresh slant on the experience of tens of thousands of expatriate Newfoundlanders who, in Pat Byrne's words, discovered that centralization meant that "there was no home to return to."[17] Al was to dedicate a significant part of his poetic effort to awakening what he recognized in himself—an unconscious intuitive knowledge of a lost community in all its often courageous, cranky, ornery and, sometimes, lonely humanity. This effort is most apparent in his poetic dramas *Rope Against the Sun* and *West Moon*, but it is directly or indirectly present in many of the poems in this collection, most notably in the earlier poems, such as "Gram Glover's Dream" and "Lines for My Grandfather Long Gone," but also in later poems, such as "The Pink, White, and Green" and "Lupins" (p. 148). These poems, which are based on a kind of homesickness for the old outport, draw on an impulse associated with collective memory.

Al's 1967 visit to Merasheen made him confront the fragility of the traditional outport culture, and this was to give a new dimension to his calling as a writer. Soon after he returned to Montreal, Al, in collaboration with Pat Byrne, began to write ballads (among them "The Government Game") which expressed the outrage he felt about the eviction of age-old communities.[18] It was surely at this time that certain ideas about the role of the poet took strong shape in his mind. These ideas provoked him to reinvent, in contemporary terms, much that was best in the imaginative and social culture of the outports. For Al, in whose mind poetry was primarily, but not exclusively, an oral art, the poet assumed several of the roles of the community singer. One of these was to be the chronicler, the voice for little local stories and shared experiences, and another was to be the celebrator of special occasions and moments. Poetry of this kind requires a style suited to an oral art, which involves measured speech (and, in more serious poems, almost incantation), alliteration and the echoing of sounds, and varied patterns of repetition and elaboration. This is a demanding art which involved Al in extensive revision. Very much the craftsman, Al strove to ensure that his poems sounded well, but he also did his best to see that they revealed their beauty and meaning with maximum clarity on the printed page.

This emphasis on clarity was part of his belief that poetry is a social form that depends on a bond between poet and reader or listener. In order to establish this kind of bond, he wanted to recreate something of the milieu of the community singers. To this end, throughout his life, he was in the practice of establishing himself in a bar or club—his studio, as it were—where he would write, entertain friends, bring in singers and arrange readings. This culminated in his organizing for years the March Hare evenings in Corner Brook, which are now part of what is virtually a provincial festival, with events occurring in several centres. Each of these occasions offers presentations that may include poetry readings, recitations and performances of folk songs and traditional music–the listeners being sustained by rabbit stew and anything from screech to spring water.

A belief in the social and shared experience of poetry—which the March Hare evenings make possible—was a facet of Al's resolve to keep alive a contemporary version of traditional Newfoundland. This belief was confirmed by his experiences as a young man. From 1968 to 1970, he was a student at St. Thomas University in Fredericton, New Brunswick, but most of his education took place in the kitchen and living room of poet Alden Nowlan, who nicknamed Al Captain Pittman.[19] From Alden, he learned to refine his poetic craft, and, from the thirsty friends at Alden's kitchen table, he learned to share poetry in a great many ways. From Alden's table, he moved in 1970 to the island community of Fogo Town, one of the few Newfoundland outports to successfully resist resettlement. Here, his experiences as a teacher confirmed his belief in the special value of outport communities. You might say that he was ready for the big move—to St. John's in 1972.

The next three years were those of his artistic coming of age, the time of the publication of his first uniformly good collection of poems, *Through One More Window* (1974), and his first play, which appeared in the same year, *Rope Against the Sun*. These were years of ferment and excitement in St. John's, a period which has sometimes been called "the little renaissance."[20] It was a time when many members of the artistic community were engaged in rediscovering and adapting traditional forms to contemporary circumstances. This was an imaginative world in which Al was immediately at home and in which he became deeply involved. He became script writer for the Ryan's Fancy television show, and he was responsible for bringing fiddlers Rufus Guinchard and Emile Benoit to a national audience.[21] At the same time, he was running the Basement Theatre, which was to welcome Tommy Sexton, Mary Walsh, Cathy Jones, Andy Jones and Greg Malone to pave the road for the popular appeal of shows like the satirical *Cod on a Stick*.

There was both give and take in the situation. Al contributed in many ways to "the general resurgence of the arts."[22] He also drew energy from the vigorous activity of poets, dramatists, painters, publishers, performers and folk and traditional musicians, whom he encountered almost every day. The early 1970s were a time of enormous energy on the musical scene, and these years saw the formation of Figgy Duff, the Red Island Band and the Wonderful Grand Band.[23] Neil Murray, Genevieve Lehr and others were to bring back from the bays to St. John's a large repertoire of traditional music and lyrics which was to be an incredible blessing to ballad singers like Pamela Morgan and Anita Best (themselves collectors). Al's beloved fiddler friend Rufus Guinchard sometimes performed in the city and was teaching much of what he knew to Kelly Russell, son of writer Ted Russell, whom Al revered so much. Chris Brooke's Mummer's Troupe was bringing topical documentary theatre to the city, while dramatist Michael Cook was creating enormously effective renderings of the torments of outport life in such plays as *The Head, Guts and Soundbone Dance, Teresa's Creed* and *Quiller*. At the same time, Al's close friend Gerry Squires had returned from Ontario to discover his own style in gnarled and stark landscapes and portraits, and Christopher Pratt and David Blackwood were creating intense images of outport and harbour life, especially in the latter's seal hunting series.[24] There can be no doubt that the poets, publishers, musicians, singers, dramatists, scholars and painters drew strength and inspiration from one another. There was a collaborative spirit in the air—a sense of belonging to and creating a common culture.

For Al, the heart of this culture lay in poetry, broadly defined. His poems reflect a passionate interest in the work of fellow poets: they include allusions, echoes, dedications and references to the work of many poet friends, to John Steffler's *Explanation of Yellow*, to David Elliot's *The Edge of Beulah* and to the poems of Enos Watts and Tom Dawe (as well as those of mainland poets Patrick Lane, Lorna Crozier, Susan Musgrave, Pat Lowther, Dennis Lee and Michael Ondaatje). But he had room in his imagination for many of the arts. He has written a moving elegy for fiddler Rufus Guinchard, "Kelly at the Graveside" (which also contains a fine tribute to Ted Russell). He has also brought the images of painters David Blackwood and Gerry Squires into his poems (for example in "Declaration of War" and "Ashes, Ashes!").

It is interesting to see in "Gram Glover's Dream" how Al employs the resources of poetry to enhance the power of David Blackwood's print, which has the same title (p. 64). Both print and poem present a time freeze of the instant when a woman turns for the last time to face the home which she is leaving forever, along with all the other members of her outpost community. The linear time sequence of poetry with its spaced verses and end-stopped lines gives an enhanced impression of the slow movement of the thinning human line streaming away from the settlement. And, at the central moment, the reader stops with Gram and the poem and is caught in the time freeze, the shocked moment when she sees "in the window a flower pot / and in it a flower bloomed open / to the day's bright light." The movement of the verse makes its own comment on the situation, the little verse in its own space forcing the reader to reflect on the discrepancy between the living flower in the deserted house and the human line streaming away to nothing.

Another intriguing aspect of Al's poems is that their apparent simplicity disguises the surprise which comes with an awakening to extra dimensions, or to a shifting perspective. One of the hallmarks of his poems is exceptional formal clarity. They are beautifully laid out. The endings are implicit in their beginnings, and the beginnings are in some way echoed in the endings. There is a precision and subtlety in the movement from line to line and from verse to verse. But very often there is also the unexpected flash, the sudden shift, or, as in "Gram Glover's Dream," the moment of sudden human insight.

Such moments can be very poignant, especially in an oral reading. I believe that the strength, simplicity and artistry of Al's poems have their origins in his primarily oral conception of poetry. The essential unit of composition for Al was the phrase (sometimes called "the measure" by American proponents of open-form poetry).[25] We see this particularly clearly in his "St Leonard's Revisited" (p. 40). Here, as if to emphasize the principle of composition, the phrases coincide with the lines. The poem opens, "we came ashore where wild flower hills tilted to the tide." I have indicated the line breaks by spaces to show how the design of the poem enhances the cadence of each individual phase, as if to allow the listener/reader to take in each of the phrases as a unit and to hear each of its syllables. In the second and third lines, consonance ("wild flower hills") and alliteration ("tilted to the tide") help to define each phrase as a unit. And the phrases are linked by verbal echoes from line to line: ashore/flower, wild/tide, hills/tilted. These have the effect of linking the lines in a manner distantly related to rhyme. The movement from line to line is an important feature of the poem in that a mnemonic principle is at work in a number of the line breaks. The poem closes with an image of the offshore fishers' close-up view of the grass paths that "led / like trap doors / to a past / they could hardly recall." The break between the second and third lines here gives the reader the sensation of being held in suspension over a trap-door, and the break also happens to be the moment of illumination in the poem.

Al's principles of composition, especially his reliance on the phrase, were very adaptable. They are evident in his beautifully designed "Lines for My Grandfather Long Gone" (p. 82). This poem turns on the speaker's memory of his mysterious experience as a child when his grandfather rang a huge rusty church bell, kept in the corner of his yard, and seemingly arrested the world's movement. Anyone who has heard the recording of this poem will remember the beautifully measured pace of Al's reading.[26] Here, the short line often extends into longer lines, but, in the case of these, Al divides them with a discernible pause and, like the Anglo-Saxon *scop* (lyrical bard), he slightly heightens the intonation of the stressed syllables so as to give shape to his phrases. The poem evokes a transforming moment in a small boy's life, presented as a time freeze. The resources of an oral poet are essential to Al's capturing the momentary quality of the experience. All the verbal echoes, refrains and repetitions combine to produce the illusion of time's standing still. The repeated line—"the yard is pale in pale light"—with its almost incantatory sound, is likely to haunt the reader's ear. A comparable effect is produced by the lines "I sit on your doorstep / waiting for something to happen." These lines recur three times, with variations, and contribute not only to the mood of expectancy but also to the auditory power of the poem. The use of repeated syllables, words, phrases and lines is very characteristic of Al, and this repetition demonstrates his affinity with oral poets. In his poems, as in many of theirs, repetition functions in at least three ways: as a mnemonic device (assisting the reader to remember), as an establisher of mood and, when variants are used, as a guide to the precise use of the imagination.

The echoing patterns of "Lines for My Grandfather" produce an almost hypnotic effect. Al creates strongly contrasting effects in many of his other poems, which are extremely varied in tone and subject matter. For example, a complete change of pace is provided by "Funeral," which consists of a single fifty-line sentence with every line being run on to the next, so as to provide a playmate's breathless version of the wonderful adventure of his friend Bubby's death (p. 99). The listener is scarcely able to draw breath as the words tumble out:

> ...everybody cried buckets
> as they should've
> especially the red eyed aunts
> and the neighbourly wives
> and twisted Norman
> once all week long any
> Hank Snow songs from his happy
> high flying swing

Al's use of a swift succession of phrases, almost without pause between lines, is a departure from his usual practice of making his pauses quite distinct. The unreflective tone created by the rapid string of lines makes its own comment on the rather grisly form that a child's innocence takes here.

In some of the teasing poems which Al wrote for close artistic friends, we are closer to the norms of his poetic practice. A case in point is his "Declaration of War," a slightly tongue-in-cheek tribute to the way the power of a painter's images can infiltrate deep into the centre of consciousness and into the heart of our domestic lives (p. 97). The effect of the poem depends, among other things, on the contrasted weighting of two kinds of phrase—one with strong looming syllables and the other with a saucy skip. In the following short passage, the first two lines are of the "looming" kind and, in the third, of a lighter kind: "every headland I see brooding / above the ocean has your ancestors / posing for pictures above it."

Al's deep affection for his gifted friends is reflected in a very different way in "Kelly at Graveside" (p. 139). In this elegy for Rufus Guinchard, the intensity of Al's feelings inadvertently create an almost bardic tone. Here, the surge of wind and grief are echoed in the surge of parallel phrases:

> In this wind-blown   wild-flowered
> fenced in meadow by the sea   this
> bleak September day   we are the silent
> sombre witnesses   to your burial
> in the black earth.[27]

The building rhythm of the phrases is enhanced by the strong alliterative stress pattern which conveys the grieving dignity of the moment. As shown in this poem, Al was exceptionally sensitive to the tonal properties of words, and he had a sixth sense for the way combinations of words created a tone appropriate to the subject. His instinctive gift for creating unity of tone was an aspect of his deep respect for the listener/reader. He so much wanted each individual to share his imaginative experience. He knew, however, that there was always an impediment to perfect communication. He was convinced that there was something inadequate about words–that they never fully expressed the poet's conception or intention.

Something of this sense of the inadequacy of language is shown by "What My Father Said about Sound," a poem which helps us to understand how strongly he was drawn to the sometimes intolerable struggle with words, its delight and its impossibility (p. 117). Perhaps the problem of "How to describe the sound of the sea" cannot "be solved." Perhaps it is true that "if ever...someone discovers / the right word.../ then there's an end to poetry and (perhaps) / even sound itself."Yet for Al, the essence of poetry lay in the striving. It may be that "the sea's sounds are the sea's alone," but it is in the attempt to find words for them that we honour what is beyond words.

In Al's best poems, the precision of words, the exactness of language, only point towards what is really inexpressible. No words are fully adequate to express the enigmatic experience of the four-year-old in "Lines for My Grandfather," and they cannot interpret the meaning of "the thinnest of smiles" on his Pop's face. No combination of Al's words can speak Shanadithit's unspeakable anguish. And in "Poem for Marilee Sleeping," even whispered words would disturb the "something" which is "so delicate" that "the slightest intrusion would shatter it" (p. 60). Even in lighter and more playful poems, like "Road to LaScie" and "One Night in Winnipeg," we are given glimpses of human secrets that words will never fathom (p. 95).

Though he did not always find it easy to do so, and knew that his attempts were never fully adequate, Al attempted to share the imaginative experiences which were most important to him. The frequent appearance of the second person "you" in his poems points to his belief that poetry is a collaborative art which flourishes in a mood of shared pleasure. When he read at poetry readings, his voice took on a flat incantatory quality–and this, and the measured pauses, created a space for his listeners. The latter could not only let the words echo in their ears, but also imaginatively reconstruct their meaning for themselves. Similarly, on the printed page, his poems are spaced in such a way as to allow the reader to take them into his or her own inner spaces. He wanted his listeners/readers to share his poet's eyeview "of all that circles below us" (p. 176), and of all the circles in which we live: personal, familial, communal, ancestral and dreaming. Surely he would also have wanted us all to celebrate poetry on a "starlit beech…beside the slap-happy sea" with "the Northern Lights" singing "in the sky" (p. 175).

—Martin Ware

End Notes

1. The "rusty nail" phrase is one that folklorist Wilfred Wareham is reported as hearing.
2. *West Moon*'s tour of Ireland was organized principally by Rex Brown and Patrick Monaghan, with the play being directed by Ken Livingstone. It was the first Canadian play to professionally tour Ireland.
3. On April 8 and 9, 2002, there was a public celebration of Al's life at the Arts and Culture Centre in Corner Brook, Newfoundland. A dramatic collage written in the last two years of Al's life, *The Moon Also Rises*, which was a prelude of sorts to *West Moon*, was given its first public performance on April 8. On the following evening, a musical tribute featuring Newfoundland and Labrador's finest traditional musicians took place in honour of Al.
4. "Prose Poem 3" in this volume, p.72 . Further references to Al's poems which appear in this book will be indicated in the text of this essay simply by page numbers.
5. Al Pittman, "The Worst Birthday Gift I Ever Gave," *Once When I Was Drowning* (St John's: Breakwater, 1978) 64.
6. Carl Leggo, "The Poet is a Poem," *A View from My Mother's House* (St John's: Killick Press, 1999) 67.
7. Quoted by Contessa Small, "A Voice of Our People," *The Humber Log* 2 Aug. 2000: 3.
8. E. J. Pratt's words cited by Adrian Fowler, "Newfoundland Poetry in the Seventies: The Context," CV II 6.3 (1982): 6.
9. Information given by Pat Byrne, personal interview, 22 May 2002; and by Anita Best, personal interview, 21 May 2002.
10. Wilfred Wareham, "The Monologue in Newfoundland," *The Blasty Bough*, ed. Clyde Rose (St John's: Breakwater, 1976) 196.
11. Byrne, personal interview.

12. Information about Al's stay in Montreal provided by Pat Byrne, personal interview; also by Adrian Fowler, personal interview, June 2001.
13. Al Pittman, "The Brown Derby," *Through One More Window* (St John's: Breakwater, 1974) 40.
14. "Al Pittman: The Only Newfoundlander to Ride with Jesse James," CBC Radio Documentary, 23 Feb. 1997.
15. Al Pittman, "Death of an Outport," in *Baffles of Wind and Tide: A Selection of Newfoundland Writings*, ed. Clyde Rose (St John's: Breakwater, 1974) 57-63.
16. "Al Pittman: The Only Newfoundlander."
17. "Al Pittman: The Only Newfoundlander."
18. According to Pat Byrne, he and Al worked together on each of the ballads, but, at the composition stage, Al wrote the words and Pat the music.
19. Patrick Toner, *If I Could Turn and Meet Myself: The Life of Alden Nowlan* (Fredericton: Goose Lane, 2000) 258.
20. Fowler, personal interview. The phrase was in fairly general use.
21. Byrne.
22. Fowler, "Newfoundland Poetry in the Seventies" 7.
23. Much of the information about artistic activity in St John's in the early seventies was given me by Adrian Fowler, personal interview. Further details were derived from "Ancient, Wild and Beautiful," CBC Television Documentary, Sept. 1999.
24. George Story, "Notes from a Berry Patch," The Blasty Bough 183.
25. See *Interviews with William Carlos Williams*: "Speaking Straight Ahead," ed. Linda Welshimer Wagner (New York: New Directions, 1976) 66-9.
26. *Newfoundland Poets: Volume 1*, selected by Des Walsh, Pigeon Inlet Productions.
27. The spacing within the lines is added in order to indicate the phrasing.

Discovering Al Pittman's Poems

AROUND THE TIME I turned eighteen, I stumbled upon Al Pittman's *Once When I Was Drowning* tucked away on a bottom shelf at the back of a now non-existent bookstore in the Avalon Mall. I was in my third year at Memorial University, and I was a recent poetry convert, rummaging for cheap copies in second-hand stores, picking through the stacks at the QEII Library. I had started writing my own poems by then, although it was something I kept to myself and something I remained secretive about for years afterwards. It's hard to pinpoint the source of that shyness now. There was an ever-present fear of failure, for starters, and an acute awareness of the gap between my ambitions and my abilities. And looming over all other insecurities was a sense of how absurd it was even to want such a thing.

These days, Newfoundland writers are regularly published nationally and internationally, finding their way onto bestseller lists and the cover of *The Globe and Mail*'s "Books Section" and prize shortlists. When I first decided to write poetry, though, there was much less obvious activity, less public celebration and acclaim. From what I could tell, writers lived elsewhere, in Britain and the United States, and, occasionally, in Montreal or Toronto. They also tended, by and large, to be long dead. I could well imagine how people would react to a kid from Buchans who got it in his mind to think himself a poet. They'd have laughed and shook their heads at the gall. And rightly so, as far as I was concerned, which is why I tended to do my scribbling behind closed doors.

It would be overstating the case to say *Once When I Was Drowning* was a life-changing experience for me. I stayed in the closet as a writer for years after I first encountered it, after all. But it would be hard to exaggerate the significance of coming upon Al's collection almost twenty years ago. Here was a contemporary local poet between the covers of his own book, a poet of this place whose plain-spoken lyricism spoke directly to my own awkward first steps as a writer. It may not have been revelatory, but it was a real and lasting encouragement. I'll always be grateful for that. And I'm equally grateful for *An Island in the Sky*, which is the place that the next generation of young writers will discover Al's poems. It's the place where those of us who already love his work will go to revisit the deceptive simplicity of his voice, his clear-eyed celebration of the ordinary, and moments like those in "Lines for my Grandfather Long Gone" when an ordinary day is lifted into a kind of heightened, almost mystical, otherness.

The world in Al's poetry is often touched by those moments of magic and wonder, but he always stopped short of suggesting anything like transcendence. From reading a piece like "Kelly at Graveside," I think he'd say if there's anything at all to eternity for him, the poems are it. And they are no small comfort. Al Pittman is no longer with us, but his poetry is a real and lasting thing.

—Michael Crummey

Textual Note

CERTAIN POEMS IN this book which are included in the selections from *The Elusive Resurrection*, *Seaweed and Rosaries* and *Through One More Window* were revised and reprinted in *Once When I Was Drowning*. We have used the revised forms of these poems as they appear in the latter collection, but we have included these poems in the selections from Al's earlier collections in order to indicate when the genesis of these poems took place. Below is a list of these poems with page numbers first corresponding to the original publication date and the original text in which these poems were published and, second, to the later publication date and the later text in which these poems were published:

FROM *The Elusive Resurrection*:

"The Border," *The Elusive Resurrection*, 15; *Once When I Was Drowning*, 42.

FROM THE POEMS IN *Seaweed and Rosaries*:

"St. Leonard's Revisited," *Seaweed and Rosaries*, 7; *Once When I Was Drowning*, 20.

"The Cost of a Good Canoe," *Seaweed and Rosaries*, 20; *Once When I Was Drowning*, 40.

"Boys at Baseball," *Seaweed and Rosaries*, 18-19; *Once When I Was Drowning*, 33.

"Guilty as Charged," originally published as "Trial" in *Seaweed and Rosaries*, 35; *Once When I Was Drowning*, 13.

"Homecoming," originally published as "Carefully Phantom Style" in *Seaweed and Rosaries*, 14; *Once When I Was Drowning*, 4.

FROM THE POEMS IN *Through One More Window*:

"Cooks Brook," *Through One More Window*, 8-9; *Once When I Was Drowning*, 65-66.

"The Echo of the Ax," *Through One More Window*, 38; *Once When I Was Drowning*, 71.

"Celebration," *Through One More Window*, 20; *Once When I Was Drowning*, 10-11.

"St. Joseph's Feastday, Fogo Island," *Through One More Window*, 13; *Once When I Was Drowning*, 51.

"Poem for Marilee Sleeping," *Through One More Window*, 48; *Once When I Was Drowning*, 72-73.

"Gram Glover's Dream," *Through One More Window*, 36-37; *Once When I Was Drowning*, 18-19.

"On the Road to LaScie," *Through One More Window*, 26-27; *Once When I Was Drowning*, 49-50.

"Shanadithit," *Through One More Window*, 17-19; *Once When I Was Drowning*, 43-46.

From
THE
ELUSIVE
RESURRECTION
1966

The Berry Pickers

Many a day we climbed
beyond the last hay-mown meadow
up the rock strewn face
where the Burnt Hills dipped
to meet the peopled valley
and as we groped our well known way
toward the summit of the first rise
to where the way was worn
and the travelin' easy
we could see
through sun-squinted eyes
(where the trail opened above us
here and there
to give the climbers their bearings)
the white flour sacks
wrapped around sun-stroked heads

There were others ahead of us
but no worry
we had our spot
and they had theirs
where the squash berries green and firm
were waiting to be picked
by counted cupfuls
and dumped into Cream of the West bags
to be toted home to the kitchen cupboard
to ripen
or to be sold at doors
for 50¢ a gallon

✦✦✦

The Border

The brook was the border.
We'd gather there on our side
above the falls
on Saturday afternoons
our pockets filled with stones
carefully selected
from the roadside gravel.

They would form up on the far side
and soon the battle would begin.
Rarely did anyone get hurt
but only because our weapons
were inaccurate at such range.
If by chance we did draw blood
we'd jump for joy
all up and down the bank
and the canyon below the falls
would resound with our victory chants.

We never knew them by name
and never cared to.
I don't know why we fought them.
The only thing they had ever done
to us was to return stone-throw
for stone-throw.

Their only offence was
they lived across the brook.

They hated us for the same reason.

❖❖❖

Baptism

How I should like
to return
to the fields
and lie a while
with new-grown hay
whipping my face
in its breeze-blown
gentle way

And stepping stones
following a living stream
in winding cataract fashion
down to the sea

And taste the salt
sprayed my way
by shore-crashing waves

And lift my eyes
to the mountains behind
my heart to the sky above

And taste once more
the sweet life
that knows no confession

And is
in itself
a sacrament of the living

◆◆◆

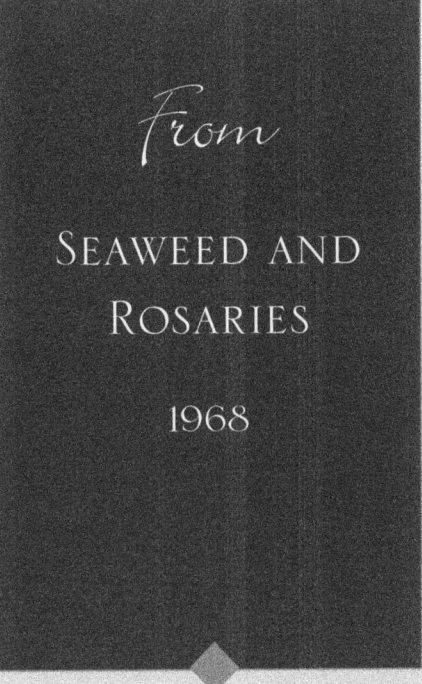

From

SEAWEED AND ROSARIES

1968

St. Leonard's Revisited

We came ashore
where wildflower hills
tilted to the tide
and walked
sad and gay
among the turnip cellars
tripping over the cremated
foundations
of long-ago homes
half buried
in the long years' grass

Almost reverently
we walked among the rocks
of the holy church
and worshipped roses
in the dead yard
and came again to the cove
as they did after rosary
in the green and salty days

And men offshore
hauling traps
wondered what ghosts
we were
walking with the forgotten sheep
over the thigh-high grass paths
that led
like trap doors
to a past
they could hardly recall

◆◆◆

The Cost of a Good Canoe

Mike and I used to talk a lot
one time about flying
in to Red Indian Lake
and canoeing all the way out.

We'd live off the land
and shoot rapids no one
has ever seen and sleep
on the river banks and fry
rainbow trout at sun-up.

We figured it'd take two weeks
to come all the way out like that
and we'd spend whole afternoons
sitting in the Port Tavern
making plans for when we'd really do it.

This summer when I went home
Mike and I talked about it all again
and went over our plans again
sitting in the same old tavern
figuring on the cost of a good canoe
and what sort of supplies to take
and what would be the best time
of the year to go.

In the meantime fifteen years had gone by
but not once while we sat there
drinking beer and making plans
was there any mention of that sad fact.

Next summer when I go home
we'll talk about that trip again
and make more plans for when
we'll really do it
and someday if we are lucky enough
we'll be old men together -
two old men who've been friends
for more than a lifetime
sitting in a tavern agreeing perhaps
how nowadays they don't make canoes
the way they used to.

♦♦♦

Going to Get Water

There was no set time for it
that I recall
and yet
as though some silent gong
had hurried us to task
in all the back yards
up and down our street
and back on the tractor road
we lifted hoops to our shoulders
took buckets in hand
and together walked out the front gates
of the tidy yards
and like a procession of armed crusaders
began our trek to the spring

Around the bend and past Art Brown's
the mechanic
where Mrs. Brown seemed always
to be sweeping kids off the front porch
and a dozen or so wrecked cars lying about
on what she called her lawn

Past Mrs. Flynn's
whose curtains were always drawn
and whose name we knew
could only be spoken in whispers
though we never knew why

Through Mrs. Pelly's back yard
where we hoped for cookies
and as often as not got them
along with a stern warning
about trampling her gooseberry bushes

Down through Jimmy Grace's field
where the horses were
and where we were forbidden to go
by our mothers
because of the barbed wire
and the manure lying all about

Over Mrs. Penney's fence
whose kids went to public school
and weren't allowed to play with us
because we were catholic

Then down through the woods
where we often built hideouts
and where Eddy Hunt always frightened us
with stories of how he'd go there at night
to meet his father
who had drowned in George's Lake five years
before

And finally down the slippery slate path
to the spring
where we'd lie on our stomachs
and take bellyfulls of the magic water
before filling up our buckets
to begin the long weary trek
back to our thirsty kitchens

◆◆◆

Boys at Baseball

Oblivious are they
to the young girls
in summer shorts
riding bikes up and down
the sidelines.

The girls would have
the players' athletic attention
reflect itself
in the mirror of their thighs
but the boys
will have none of it.

Their minds this year
are given over to baseball
and the girls may as well
find some sport
of their own.

All that matters now
is the man on first
the pitcher's sly eye
the certain possibility
of a double play.

Little do the girls
in their innocence know
that all the long white nights
between now and next summer
it won't be the smack of the bat
or the long throw home

but vague visions of themselves
riding bare-thighed
all over the outfield
that will have these same boys
tossing and turning
in their hot winter beds.

♦♦♦

GUILTY AS CHARGED

He had come to Port aux Basques
to look for work, got involved
with the wrong woman, got into a fight
and killed a man.

For six days he sat
through his trial – the pleas,
the examinations and cross examinations,
the endless testimony, the exhibits,
the arguments, the judicial attention to detail
and the constant debate about things
that seemed to have nothing
to do with him.

Today, when the verdict was read
and the sentence passed, he looked
like he knew the worst of his punishment
was over, looked like he'd be glad
to get out of that courtroom, glad finally
to be locked up out of sight
where he wouldn't have to sit ever again
in front of all those people
feeling like some kind of fool.

♦♦♦

Searston Beach

Now
in the middle of winter
with the wind
sweeping drifts
around our back door
I think
of the beach at Searston
where last summer
we ran hurdles
over the waves
and watched
how they'd roll
all the way to the old dead tree before
going back
to take another run at it
and how
we'd sit off shore
and let the surf
tumble
us up
the beach
like bundles
of tired seawood
where we'd lie
spent like lovers
leaving our limbed impressions
in the sand
while the surf
regathered itself
to come again
smoothing away all signs
of our easy summer pleasures

❖❖❖

Angels

What if I went out right now
and made angels
in the snow
would people think I've gone mad
or would they see the truth
of it
that it's a game
we used to share
once when angels
were so real
they'd (once we made them)
take flight out of the snow
and hover all over the back yard
their white wings beating so fast
they'd shower feathers
for us to chase
and catch laughing on our tongues

♦♦♦

Homecoming

Carefully, quietly like a thief
I steal toward the bed where you
are sleeping. The serene sound
of your breathing warns me well
you sleep in some sort of peace,
are oblivious to my dark arrival.

Not wanting to wake you out of
whatever warm world you breathe in,
I slide as slow as a glacier into bed,
wrap myself in that most familiar,
most welcome of all the spaces
I so bravely, so cautiously inhabit.

The lovely heat of your hot body
burns me all over in the darkness.
I thrust gently forward and bend
touching my dry mouth to the curve
of your back. Then turn, curled,
to let the night swallow me down.

❖❖❖

From

THROUGH ONE
MORE WINDOW

1974

Cooks Brook

At the pool where we used to swim
in Cooks Brook
not everyone had guts enough
to dive from the top ledge

not that it would have been
a difficult dive
except for the shelf of rock
that lay two feet below the surface
and reached quarter of the way out
into the width of the pool

one by one the brave few of us
would climb the cliff to the ledge
and stand poised
ready to plunge headfirst
into the dark water below
and always there was that moment
of terror
when you'd doubt that you could
clear the shelf
knowing full well
it would be better to die
skull smashed open in the water
than it would be to climb
backwards down to the beach

so always there was that moment
when you prayed for wings
then sailed arms outspread into the buoyant air

what you feel is something
impossible to describe
as the water parts like a wound
to engulf you
then closes just as quickly
in a white scar where you entered

and you are surprised always
to find yourself alive
following the streaks of sunlight
that lead you gasping to the surface
where you make your way
leisurely to shore
as though there had been nothing to it
as though it was every day of the week
you daringly defied the demons
who lived so terribly
in the haunted hours of your sleep

◆◆◆

Big City Skyline

When James Dean
was the rebel without a cause
and Marlon Brando the wild one
we'd take the long cut home from school
because living
in a small town as we did
the foundry yards
provided the only sensible background for our wellington boots
and black leather jackets

even for ten minutes only
climbing the oil barrels
jumping the high solid board fence
going down alleyways
we were
no more
no less
than our deliberate uniforms
said we were

◆◆◆

The Echo of the Ax

My father tells me of the time
he put his hand
on the chopping block
and dared his brother
to cut it off

and whack
just like that
he did it
and my father remembers
the blood on the steel blade
and his mangled hand
hanging barely
by a thread of skin
and he remembers too
how his brother looked
after he'd done it
in that moment
when the whack of the ax
still echoed about the yard

and he recalls
with a heavy breath
how he felt inside
having made his brother
a most amazed victim
of his weird and private fantasies

❖❖❖

Celebration

Driving along route three
to Fredericton
for my young brother
the first time out of his town
out of his province
the first time on his own
it is a day of beginnings
for me aware now
of the manhood he assumes
it is an end of kind

not thinking any of this
just driving along nohow
we spy an apple tree
with fruit growing red
against the blue New Brunswick sky

we aren't hungry
have no appetite for apples
but stop anyway
climb the twisted trunk
Shake the apples off
gather them in bushels
filling the back seat of the car
to a useless limit

the apples are rough
and pitted black on the skin
they are bitter to the taste
and difficult to swallow

what we don't throw
at telephone poles in passing
we leave to rot on the back seat
yet our orchard thievery
is no futile act

it is an act of the blood
two brothers in a farmer's field
nowhere in New Brunswick
celebrating their brotherhood
their tribal communion
beneath the pale end
of one year's summer sky

◆◆◆

St. Joseph's Feastday, Fogo Island

1

Through this window
the iced over harbour
shimmers in spring sunlight
and sometimes
if you look closely
you can almost
see it melting

2

Kyran playing in the yard
has thrown off
one of her mittens
takes up a handful of mud
and squeezes it
smiling to herself
as it oozes out between her fingers
with the sun shining
from her blue eyes
and her hair blowing
in this first spring wind

3

Potholes and puddles
and water running everywhere
and mud
and sunshine and warm wind
and two old lovers laughing

◆◆◆

Her Portrait of Me

Until today
I'd been nothing more
than a lovable scribble
that's you daddy
that's you she'd say
quite certain that I'd never know otherwise
today however without any fuss
she drew me with a head
and two bulging eyes
a splash of a nose
a lopsided mouth
and whiskers going every which way
and when she was finished
made no announcement of any kind
but slyly left it lying around
where I'd have to see it
while she waited nearby
ready to measure my reaction
not quite sure I'd find it
as pleasing a portrait
as the scribbles she had grown to realize
I loved

❖❖❖

Poem for Marilee Sleeping

Most of this one day together
is already spent
the laundromat and supermarket
took up most of it
and then there was the trip
to the farmer's market for eggs
and the tidying up around
that you had to do

those were the major expenditures
somewhere in between
other piles of minutes
went without notice
much the way the bits and pieces
of a ten dollar bill go
once you've broken it into change

but now finally
you are deep asleep on the chesterfield
and I am silent at the kitchen table
with a bottle of wine
and pretty near a full pack of Pall Malls

the glad yelps of children playing
are gone with the daylight
and there is no noise now
of traffic or of trains shunting in the night
quiet only filters through the screen window
the moon is barely visible over the elms
down on George Street
and finally at this late hour of the day
there is something suddenly real
about our togetherness

something so delicate
it seems the slightest intrusion
like if you were to wake up
or the wind began to rise
would shatter it
send it fragmented once more
to distances beyond our reach

◆◆◆

Island Estate at St. Andrew's

Approaching the house
along the old carriage road
that leads from the tidal bar
you expect to be greeted at the door
by some monstrous hunchbacked caretaker

you expect naturally
to be led by candlelight
into the dark interior
where the house itself
like that of Usher
will drive you mad
or to your death
long before daylight comes again

you feel
that since you are here at all
your fate is sealed
like a coffin
and forevermore you will be
one insignificant mention
in a story no one will believe

but as you walk
stepping carefully up the steps
to the main entrance
there is no one to meet you
the house is locked tight
the grass threatens the path
to the garden gate
and the only sound
is that of the seagulls
swirling high in the sky
overhead

from there on the top step
standing in deep shadow
your back turned
to the great dark door
observe what perfect patterns
the bright whitecapped waves make
as they glisten silver in the sunlight
all the way to the thin horizon
and beyond

♦♦♦

Gram Glover's Dream
(from a picture of the same name by David Blackwood*)*

A long thin line
thinner and thinner as it goes
becomes a dot
disappears out where there is nothing

These are the islanders
leaving their island

huddled into the wind
they are going away

out where there is nothing
they have gone away to nothing

the long thin line winds away
in an endless swirl of snow

at the end of the line
turned to the wind
she stands looking back

if she had been farther up the line
she could have been spared this instant

but where she is
at the end of it
she is forced to confront
face to face
the final moment of their going

in a second
when this scene unfreezes
she will turn
become again the last of the line

will turn and walk away
will become nothing in the windy distance

in this instant however
she is frozen where she is

solidified against the wind
she faces the familiar house

on the window a flower pot
and in it a flower bloomed open
to the day's bright light

outside everything is frozen still
everything except the wind

and the wind's white howling
there is something suddenly real

◆◆◆

On the Road to LaScie

Ahead of me and to the left
I see a twisted figure
dancing in the dust
and when the swirling brown cloud
scatters in the air about his head
I see it is a man
an old man making fists
with one hand and hurling them
like a punch-drunk prize fighter
at a truck disappearing now
over the next hill

with his other hand
he is waving me down
and I pull over to see what's the matter
not because I'm naturally kind
to strangers on the road
but because there is something
frantic something of an emergency
in his wild and dusty dance

I have visions of his wife or son
or someone lying in the ditch
bleeding and broken
a hit and run case I think
wondering how I'll handle it
knowing well my mind's weakness
for the sight of blood.

There's been no accident however
no hit and run no body in the ditch
all he wants is a lift
to the next village
his widowed sister called
and asked him to come down
to cut some firewood for her
she has five kids but none
old or strong enough to cut wood

her husband drowned last spring
when he ran his boat up on White Sail Rock
coming in from the island
one night blind drunk
so now she's left alone
with her kids and no one
to cut firewood
so twice a week he goes down there
to help her out

curses her dead husband
every step of the way
slays him again
with every angry swing of the ax

❖❖❖

Faith Healer

They come from as far away
as Stephenville Crossing
to this tent
this temple
hobbling
bent
broken
pock marked
the whole ignoble mess
of west shore humanity
crammed into canvas
waiting
hoping
praying
that this time perhaps
God willing
their turn will come
and why not
haven't they seen miracles before

wasn't it this same man
this saint
who last year
laid hands upon a cripple
and God Almighty justlikethat
weren't the crutches thrown off
and didn't the fellow begin to dance
praising God all up and down the aisles

and hadn't they heard about the cures
last week at North Sydney too
hadn't the posters proclaimed it all
and wasn't this the self same man
and wasn't it only right
that perhaps tonight God willing
they'd leave their own
crutches and wheelchairs
pain and twist
behind them

and if they weren't chosen
for miracles tonight
then wouldn't there always be next year
to look forward to
and perhaps then God willing…

◆◆◆

Prose Poems

1.

Walking the beach, taking pleasure in the wind, I come upon two boys with spears. They are following the flatfish as they move along the shore out of the bay into the river's mouth.

Every few minutes they strike, bringing the fish up wiggling on the spiked heads of their homemade weapons. To get them off, they stand on them, pull the spears out with bits of fish flesh on the barbs, and go on, leaving each fish to flap patterns of his death in the windswept sand.

"Why do you do that?," I ask.
"Because," he replies.
"Do you eat them?"
"No."
"Do anything with them?"
"No."
"Then why do you do it?"
"Because they're no good for nothing."
"Just flatfish," the other one says.
"And besides, it's fun."

They pass on up the shore and leave me standing bewildered in my thirtieth year.

Down the beach the boys are singing. Sometimes it is hard to tell their voices from the sound the wind is making.

2.

I'm driving back to Corner Brook to pick up Marilee and Kyran to bring them back to the house I rented for us in a place called The Lord's Cove. A small house, empty except for a daybed in the kitchen and the biggest, ugliest oil stove I've ever seen, but comfortable, or will be at least, once Marilee puts her hand to it.

She'll probably be disgusted with me when we return and she sees the bean juice and mustard stains by the daybed where I ate lunches sitting on the floor all week.

I'm no sooner on the ferry to Carmanville when this fellow who's one of the crew comes up to me and asks me if I've got a beer to give him because he's suffering the worst hangover he's ever had and otherwise wouldn't ask me outright like that in a month of Sundays. So I give him a Dominion out of the half dozen I took along for the trip across the water and he sits on the deck behind my truck and drinks it down in one gulp flinging the bottle back over his head into the foaming white wake of the ferry.

Thanks Fred, he says and I wonder why he thinks my name is Fred as he moves forward up the deck to disappear among the rows of cars and coca-cola trucks.

I take out a beer for myself, open it with the
safety belt buckle and fall back to thinking how
good it will be to get back to The Lord's Cove
with Marilee and Kyran and all our stuff and not
have to eat dry crackers and mustard pickles for
breakfast and not have to go to bed at nine because
it's too cold to stay up longer and for them to be
there when I come home at noon or in the evening or
whenever.

But at the rate this ferry's moving, it's a long
ways to Corner Brook and back.

3.

I also have begun poems to all my dead friends

but I've never been able to get beyond the first
line. As though to go on, to finish, would be
to admit the fact of the matter.

Something like maybe chipping in with skilled
precision the last digit of the last date on
your own gravestone.

Nobody not quite mad enough could do it with the
steadiness of hand the craft requires.

4.

In the black of night the news has come to us.
Two boys from Back Cove lost in the fog. They
are out on the water in an open boat and the
Lord knows there's nothing worse than fog.

The bells have brought everyone out of doors.
They huddle in groups along the fences, in the
middle of the road, and around the well. The
fog envelops them.

They do not talk in whispers but still there is a
distinct lowering of voice as though they were
afraid to speak out too loud, afraid they might
somehow muffle the boom of the invisible bells
ringing out from invisible steeples.

There is talk of bonfires along the hillside and
word now that the boats have gone out. There is
talk of a gale warning and there are names mentioned
and sympathies declared and possibilities considered.

It could be they got ashore on one of the islands.
It could be they've been picked up already. It could
even be that they might be right out there in the
cove within ring of the bells.

There is no suggestion that the worst has happened.
The bells ring as vigorously now as when they began.
Men are beginning to cut boughs for the fires and
news is passed that more boats have gone out now to
join the search.

The people remain huddled. Not one of them stands anywhere alone. They talk in lowered voices. The bells boom into the fog and over on the south side there is the first flicker of flame. The bonfires have begun.

We turn toward home to wait it out listening each footstep of the way for a sudden silence in the night. Waiting for that moment when word is passed uphill to the churches, when bell ropes are released from aching hands and left to swing giddily in their damp chambers like nooses relieved of their dreadful burden after a hanging.

♦♦♦

Brimstone Head

Out on the outer edge of Brimstone Head
                              you can
                              lean on
                              the wind
              hold there for one second
                            two three
                              four maybe
                              five maybe
snap back
before the wind slacks up
                        breathe deep

                    look down at
                            the
                            sea
                            and
                            the
                            rocks
                            and the
                            gulls hunting
                            for crabs hundreds
                            of feet dead below and
                            breathe again and consider

        what if the wind
        had swung around
        backed off a bit
        or suddenly died

whether you go back by the path to Back Cove
or down the Shag Rock side
and though you keep your feet firmly
on the ground looking

out for roots and
fallen rocks and slippery places
you walk knowing you
walk with angels
angry on either side

it is something you'll do only once
between here and wherever it is you're bound
and   then   only   if

♦♦♦

Shanadithit

What I know of you is only
what my grade seven history book
told me.
That you were young when they caught you.
That your people lived in deerhide houses.
That they changed your name to Nancy.
That you died soon after.
That you were the last of the Beothuks.

You probably didn't know that
did you?
That you were the last of your people.
That when you went there was no one
to take your place.
I suppose you died thinking
there were uncles and cousins
with toothaches and babies
that there were hunters,
young men you'd like to be with,
coming home game-laden to campfires
on the shore of the lake
your executioners call Red Indian.

You didn't know
you'd end up in my grade seven history book
did you?

And when you died your lonely death,
when the white disease put an end to you,
you didn't know that all these years
beyond your decay I would long
to be with you, to tell you
I wouldn't forget. You didn't know
that I would have kissed you
and cried when you went.

Of course that has all to do
with my own images of you and they are
much too mixed up with technicolor movies
and my own boyish musings.

I see you are beautiful as Debra Paget
who played the role of an Indian girl
in a movie I barely remember.
I can't see you, no matter how hard
I try, mud-caked and offensive smelling.
I can't see you groaning and twisting
on the floor of your smokey mamateek
locked in any embrace with your rough
raw-boned cousins.

I see you
(and I know this is all wrong)
leaning over a blue pool. The sun
filters through the alders
and sends little shivers of light
bouncing off your golden thigh
where your beautifully embroidered dress
(like the one marked yours in the St. John's museum)
parts to let you bend.
Your reflection looks up to me
from the still water and your eyes

are two hollows deeper than any this brook
could fill. The eyes of a martyr,
of one who waits patiently for death
knowing that beyond all kindred deaths
yours will matter most.
Yet in all this there is a sadness
about you for you had not always
consented to your martyrdom. Before this,
before it had all been revealed to you
through witchcraft and religion,
you had wished rather that I would walk
buckskinned into your forest and take you
upstream to a place the shaman
and the gods had ordained for us.
And there, in an eternity of summers,
we would have loved each other gently
in the brook-cooled summer sun.

That dream, of course,
(though it pleases me that you had it)
was entirely impossible. For you had
to die as you did, you had to be the last
of your people before I could love you
at all.

I admit now
(putting this poem aside)
that my love for you has nothing
to do with you. Not as you were
or might have been in those few
of your own dead-end days.
For in those days surely my affection
would have been given over to some
Newfoundland lass with fair hair
and delicate English-pink skin.

There might have been times then when I
would have impressed her with stories
of how I raided your village, killed
your cousin, and laughed heartily
all the way home.
The workman who destroyed your grave
to build his portion of road
did not know what he was doing, did
not know that I would have knelt
in awe at that spot loving you
and condemning your death all in one prayer.
He did not know he ruined forever
my one chance to come close to you.
And therefore what is he guilty of
but depriving me of one singular
and pitiful indulgence? One moment
in my history when I could have knelt
over your fleshless remains and said
"Shanadithit, I love you." What did he
do but save you the agony of one more lie?
Lie easy in your uneasy peace girl
and do not, do not, forgive those
who trespass against you.

◆◆◆

From

Once When I Was Drowning

1977

Lines for My Grandfather Long Gone

I keep one memory only
of you.

I am four
and slightly shy.

You are anciently old
and brave among cows.

It is afternoon.
The yard is pale in pale light.

I sit on your doorstep
waiting for anything to happen.

You unhook the gate,
stroll through, hook
it again and stroll straight
to the old church bell hanging
heavily rusted in the corner
of the yard.

You reach out
and pull the rope.

The bell booms over the village,
booms over the sea, the hills,
the hayfields, and up into the heavens.

The yard is pale in pale light.

You stand quietly still.
Nothing moves except your arm,
your hand on the rope.

I sit on your doorstep
waiting for something to happen.

The bell booms.
In the field the cows
stop chewing. They stand
in the still hay like pathetic statues
their tails bronzed in absurd geometry.

On the sea the perpetual waves
roll motionless in their rhythmic run
to the beach. They tilt in poised
suspension above the still suspended swell.

In the sky the frivolous birds
halt in their hurried flight. They hang
like tiny black moons stationary
and still in the pale heavens.

I sit still as stone
on your doorstep watching.

Your hand on the rope stops.

The bell stops.

The field, the sea, the sky
thrive again in a confusion of movement.

I sit on your doorstep watching.
I wonder what in the world has happened.

You come strolling down
from the corner of the yard,
the thinnest of smiles upon your mouth.

You touch your ancient hand
gently to my bewildered head.
You pass me by and go into the house,
the door closing quietly behind you.

❖❖❖

Poem for a Young Man Who Froze to Death Down North, Nov. '77

You were one easily measured
mile from home when you died.

Some say the sensation
of freezing to death
is one of warmth.

You lie down.
You get very warm.
You die.

For your sake
I hope they are right
and for now I won't ask
them how they know.

I remember my hands
freezing in my mitts
when I was a boy.
I remember tears freezing
on my face all the way home.
I remember choosing any death
but yours.

Now, because I cannot rid
myself of the thought of you
lying, dying, and dead
in the snow, I like to think
you had a better death
than most.

A warm, white, blanketed,
sleepy death like rabbits
must have, giving up to old age
in winter, or polar bears
snuggled down to die dreaming
among glowing heaps
of arctic ice.

♦♦♦

I Leave My Prayers

To you, my friend, whom
I must leave here in a hospital
lying because I must fly
within the hour to a city
I live in but have nothing
to do with, I leave my prayers.

They may not make you well
or even comfortable.
They will certainly not cause
your fear to evaporate
into this sterile white air
and they will be useless
when it comes to nightmares
and times you wake up
crying in the dark.

Outside it is cold and raining,
not a good night to be going anywhere
but go I must because you are
only one of the choices I've made
and now must live with.

I would not go
if it were possible not to
and I would leave you
good health and comfort
and hope and happiness
if I could.

But because it is all I can do
I go and leave you my prayers.

❖❖❖

Old Soldiers

These are feeble men.
Their beer glasses tremble
when they lift them to drink.
They rise unsteadily from their chairs
and walk an hour's walk to the washroom.
When they return they forget
for a while where they sat.
They don't say much to each other
or more than hello to anyone else.

Certainly they are men who carry
inside and out the scars of war.
They wear their soldierhood like uniforms.
Yet they lived also years before their wars
and made it through to survive
all this crippling time since.

It is easy enough to imagine
their memories bombarded and bandaged
with the stuff of war. With barbwire
and trenches and shrapnel. With gunfire
and troops and the stench of death.
But you would be dead wrong to think it.
It is something other than war
that's brought them to this grim silence.

The one for instance who's intently
smoking his unlit pipe. The one
whose eyes are turned inward and away.
I'll tell you what he sees.

He sees himself lying quiet
and warm on the edge of a hayfield.
A young woman's hand strokes
his young body and a slender voice
lying by his side whispers his youth's beauty
to a passive summer sky.

Now he looks again and sees
his young son come tumbling down
a green hill to greet him. He lifts
the boy to his shoulders and carries
him weightless to a white house on the hill.
At the door of the house his wife
smelling of flour and cloves waits
eagerly in awe of his indifferent love.

Because you see me sitting
before you this side of middle age
and clearly unsoldiered you ask me
how I know these things. Don't let
appearances fool you. We old soldiers
are expert in the art of camouflage.

It is not the forgotten fact of war
that brings us daily to this tavern.
We come because it is a short stroll
from anywhere and the beer is cheap.
Because this place is as good as any
to sit in and remember while we wait
patiently to forget.

❖❖❖

DRIFTWOOD

Perfection is an elusive end, found
only, I suppose, in some kind of death.
Take driftwood for instance. Cast high
and dry in the uppermost reaches
of the beach. Take this piece here. Notice
its perfection. Its perfect age. Shape.
Colour. Texture. Its exact immobility.

Imagine it sometime growing. Out of the earth.
Imagine it with odour. Motion. And a desire
to be complete. Imagine it part of something
other. A branch. Limb. Trunk. Root. Imagine it
moving in the earth. In the wind. Imagine it
upright under the weight of an endless winter.
Gleaming green in summer rain. Imagine its
unimaginable wooden death. Its inevitable retreat
to the sea. Imagine it floating. Sinking. Rising.
Moving. Forever untouched by decay. Moving
always in mystery toward its own elusive end.

Imagine us someday standing here beyond
the long tide's ingenious reach observing
our own finality. A grey portion of bone
ignored perfectly by insects. Oblivious
perfectly to the heat of the sun. The shift
of sand. The grip of ice. Rain. Wind.
Time. Imagine us cast up here in perfect
communion with this driftwood. How we'd
stand amazed in awe of our own completion.
How we'd stand. Amazed. In awe. Of our own
immutable and indescribable perfection.

◆◆◆

Song Also
(a reply to Pat Lowther)

Take me to your island.
I'll speak so softly
you'll have to feel my words
whispering on your skin.
Coming from my own island
I know very well how sound
carries across water.
I'll come in the blackest night
of the year and walk with you
through the twisted trees
to the sea.
And we'll collect
whatever jewelled creatures
you want to wish up
out of the onyx ocean.
We'll lie side by side on the sand
and let the sky touch us
where it will.
I'll wear my warmest skin
and follow whatever you go.
And I'll speak only silence
if you'll take me.

◆◆◆

Confession

What is there left
to say, now
that I've lied to you
all night long?

How my fingers curled
too tightly in your hair
was a small lie, hardly
a lie at all, but my hand
quivering in yours
like an egg anxious to give
birth, that was certainly
a lie, and my mouth's
gentle journey across
your breast was a lie,
and my eager hand's slow
search for your flesh
beneath the blankets, that
was a lie, and my holding
you desperately, like my life
depended on it, that was
a lie too.

And now this stark morning
what lies are there left
to tell, except the one lie
I must speak to you with words?

I speak it now, give you
the words without guilt:

I don't ever want to stop
lying to you.

◆◆◆

Winter '72
(for Kevin Miller)

Low under the crook of the hill
snugged away in your sea room house
we come together crewlike and contented
with the whole unwholesome host of our fantasies

outside and above the boiling cove
above the age-old fish-storied stages
(resisting still in their trembling old age
the never-say-die seaweeded sea)
the sky crawling gulls claw
at the white confusion of the whistling wind
scratch their screeching frenzy
on the impenetrable windwall of our alliance

cozied now in the elbow of your armchair
I perceive the corrupting blue day's dawn
creeping like cats into your seaside yard
and curling comfortable in the lap of your living room
consider time's timeless quarrel
with the poor ever orphaned earth

within this room this wished for dawnless day
the only colours are those of my own invention
like you yourself sitting stone blue
behind the veiled blueness of your cigarette smoke
curling now like cobras
about your martyred head
like me sitting as colourless
as a decomposed king
wishing for you a spangled princess
sprawled weeping among her veils
begging your forgiveness

◆◆◆

THE PIGEON ON THE GATE
(for Rufus Guinchard)

Well hell!
Old friend.
Old fiddler.

Hawkes Bay was never like this
was it?

What with the lost women,
the porno shops,
the blue movies,
the concert violinist practising
down the hall.

Not much like the old logging camps
is it my friend?

Not much like your trapline country?

Not much like anything is it?

You and me
(you the 77 year old fiddler
come to sudden fame
me the 37 year old poet
come to nothing much)
here on the edge of a bed
in the Chelsea Inn wondering
how we might get the violinist
to join us.

❖❖❖

One Night in Winnipeg
(for Pat Byrne)

One night in Winnipeg
while the fiddler was playing
and people were talking
and drinking and singing
and the desk clerk dozed
between complaints
and the city outside the hotel
went about its usual business
and the sky blackened
over the prairie
I watched you melting ice cubes
in a beer bucket

you may say ice melts
on its own in hot hotel rooms
but that wouldn't fool me
because I saw clearly
how you'd select a cube
and stab it with your eye
like a heron stabbing fish
and how the cube would melt
visibly and much faster
than the others

then you'd select another
and again in seconds it'd be gone
and then another until you sat
sadly looking into a green pail
of water

I don't know what you were thinking
at the time but I know
only two things that can put the power
of fire into your eyes like that
one is anger
the other the wish that someone
would do to you what you did
to the ice cubes
and come to think of it
I don't remember you being there
when it came time to say goodnight
and now they tell me
no one has seen or heard tell of you
since

◆◆◆

Declaration of War
(for Gerry Squires)

With your pens your pencils
charcoals inks temperas and oils
and with your artist's arrogance
you alter my world

I can no longer look
at the Ferryland Downs and see
anything but your intricate ink marks

They have replaced forever
the stunted spruce the crags
and rocky ravines

every headland I see brooding
above the ocean has your ancestors
posing for pictures upon it

every crucified christ's head
is the underside of a jellyfish
tentacles haloing like sunrays
around its pink middle

every oldtimer and smiling child
turns in the wink of an eye
into one of your stark sketches

I expect one of these days
when you've transformed the rest of the world
you'll invade the privacy of my refrigerator
and leave me starving to death
on a diet of acrylic salads

or you'll come after my wife and daughters
with your miraculous arsenal
and leave me lonely the rest of my life
living with a family of pale portraits

so if you wake some morning soon
and find your brushes broken
your paints splattered about your house
you'll know I've taken the offensive

it is dear friend
a matter of survival

◆◆◆

Funeral

When Bubby died
the whole world turned
into a splendid adventure
and everybody cried buckets
as they should've
especially the red eyed aunts
and the neighborly wives
and twisted Norman who didn't
once all week long nasal any
Hank Snow songs from his happy
high flying swing
and people gathered together
in lovely little groups
around Mr. Rideout's confectionery store
and wondered whispering why he died
and little Gary Keough
who was with him when it happened
said secretly that the bogey man
pushed him over the cliff
and Mrs. Borden said loud enough
for his mother to hear
that he was a miserable little liar
and that he probably pushed him
over himself and some people said
it was just an accident most likely
and a very sad sad one too
him being only five and a half
and deaf 'n dumb all his little life
and Mr. Pelley said he got some fright
when he pulled him from the water
because he thought he was just a old onion bag
and he said he got a terrible fright
when it turned out to be Bubby

and there was never a sadder
more wonderful wake than Bubby's
because he was afterall my dead friend
who I used to play with
just about every day
including the day he died
and his funeral when they threw
handfuls of dirt in on top
of the sparkling white coffin
was the most glorious sad thing
in the whole whopping wide world
and nobody in all of Buckle's Valley
talked of anything else
for the most marvellous long time
until Jimmy Pinsent
got run over by his father's truck
and he died too.

♦♦♦

April

The child sits hunched
in the corner of the yard.
The snow floating slowly down
gathers on his knees, his shoulders,
his bowed head. Gathers on the woodpile,
the fence, the chopping block.

The child sits still,
waiting to be erased.

All the voices in the world
could call him now and he
wouldn't hear.

He's discovered
almost what it's like
to be nothing.

The snow floats slowly down.
The child sits hunched in the corner
of the yard. Companion and almost kin
to the woodpile, the fence, the chopping block.

❖❖❖

Angelmaker

My daughter is too young yet,
too small, too encumbered
with the weight of her snowsuit
to make angels in the snow.
She can fall back ok and spread
her arms and legs and scoop
the angel shape out just right.
And while she's lying there
in her purple prison looking
perplexed, there's a perfect
angel lying beneath her
in the snow. But when she tries
to rise, she ruins it. It becomes
just another indefinable dent
in the snow full of fists
and knees and bums. Sometimes
I help her out by picking her
up. That way leaving her angel
all in one piece. But this
doesn't please her. She won't
be happy until she makes her angel
all by herself. Until her angel
takes flight out of the snow
and ascends homeward to whatever
heaven thrives shining in the
loveliest regions of her sleep.

❖❖❖

From

DANCING
IN LIMBO

1993

Atlantis

Now at run-off time
the river sleeps deep
in the dark woods, drowning
in its depths my daughters'
fond places. Fish swim
in paths they danced along
last summer. Eels swarm
where they played out
the truths of their childhood.

A week from now, the river
will be back in its own bed.
The paths and clearings
in the woods will sprout
new grass and curled ferns.
My girls will be there
as lovely and familiar
as flowers.

Today their deep wooded world
is the haunt of gilled things.
Because they know every twist
and turn of season here, they
are not disturbed by this.
They play at the water's edge
and wait patiently, with love,
for the turning world to give
them back their little lost
Atlantis.

♦♦♦

Goodnight Kiss
(for Emily)

My daughter's note (scrawled
in chalk on a toy blackboard)
reads: Mom,
      I'm gone to sleep.
      Please kiss me goodnight.
            Emily

She knows she'll still be asleep
when her mother comes home. She does not ask
to be awakened, does not expect to be aware.
When morning comes she will not inquire
whether or not she received her kiss.
She might ask her mother if she saw her note.
She might want to know that.
But for the meantime she is sound asleep
upstairs waiting to be kissed. And what
if the kiss were not given? What then?
She'd not know it. Or would she?
Is there, in a kiss, some transmission
of love that penetrates sleep, goes straight
to the waiting heart? Or could it be
my daughter requests only that ritual
prevail? I think not. I think she is so open
to give and receive of all she feels
that sleep, no matter how sound, how deeply
steeped in dreams, cannot keep that kiss
or its absence unknown to her. She will not
wake up. But she will know.

So, just in case, before I go to bed
I leave (where it cannot be overlooked)
a note printed in very large letters.
The note reads: Marilee,
        I am gone to bed.
        Emily left a note for you
        on her blackboard. After
        you've answered her plea,
        please do the same for me.
                Al

◆ ◆ ◆

Grace before Meals

There.
Supper's done.
Ready to be served.
Late as usual.
Insubstantial perhaps.
But ritual observed.
The most important thing of it all
gone unneglected again.
A simple task of kitchen and cupboard ware
orchestrated into some semblance of service.
Now my daughter and I
will sit down alone together
to dine.
I will love her
across the width of this table
and beg her forgiveness
for every morsel she will endure.
And she will give me thanks.
We could do with a choir
a host of friends
lovers or angels
to sing this grace
before this meal.
But this is how it goes.
This is how we slide forward
one immeasurable moment at a time.
For this we dine together
on our knees.

❖❖❖

Boxing the Compass

The sky is slate grey
threatening rain.
Wind south-southeast.
Maybe more south-by-south-southeast.

The difference could be crucial.

When I was a child
my father took me
around the compass
hundreds and hundreds
of times.

"Boxing the compass" he called it.

Evenings at the kitchen table
he'd draw the compass
on a piece of paper
and have me memorize by name
the thirty-two points from
north to north-north-west-by-north.

We didn't live on the sea then.
And his own ocean-going days
were all long gone.
He drove a car to work.
I walked to school.
The mud-rutted road defined his direction.
The brambled short-cut path defined mine.

But evenings after supper
as though my life depended on it
he'd sit me down beside him

where with a plate from the cupboard
and my school ruler he'd draw
the compass for the thousandth time.

Dusk after dusk
he'd test my memory
until I walked around
inside the house
on the road
in the fields
up the brook
with the compass
spinning this way and that
inside my head.

And sitting in school
through multiplication and long division
through the Ten Commandments and the Beatitudes
through the Crusades and the War of 1812
through the conjugation of latin verbs
through the poems of Bliss Carman and Pauline
Johnson
I wound around the compass like a clock
gone giddy with turning.

In the middle of his middle age
I bought my father a boat and a compass.
We moored her in the shelter of a small cove
where she could come to no harm
while at rest between her little league voyages
up and down the unhazardous shore.
But even when she was tied up
going nowhere bouncing gently
up and down and around her mooring
I'd see from back aft

my father in the wheelhouse
standing spread-legged.
The wheel in his calloused grip.
His eyes glued to the compass.
And I wondered then
if he was out somewhere
in a bank of fog on the Grand Banks
rolling in a south-east wind
remembering.

Once upon a time
in a fog bank on the Grand Banks
his younger brother went overboard.
And though they searched all night
they couldn't find him.
When the fog lifted at daybreak
they looked again.
But no luck.

My father and my uncle
their brother gone
forever to "the grey seas under"
took their course
and headed south-south-west-by-west
to Boston.

His boat is long gone
to the sand and the seaside grass.
But I still have the compass
he used to navigate his last voyage
to nowhere.
It sits on a stand
in a corner of my living room.
I check it often
each and almost every day.

◆◆◆

Passing through St. Jude's

P.S. Say me to your friends.

That's how my mother ends
all her unanswered letters
to me.

Some of my friends
find it a strange phrase.
But it's only one of many
she's never discarded
from the many times
the places
or any of the lives
she's lived in.

Near here
there's a place called
St. Jude's.

It's a length of residential highway
between here and the nearest airport.

It used to be known as
The Chute.

But some parish priest
in his benevolence
decided the people who lived there
in their tar-paper houses
with their very many children
deserved the intercession of
The Patron Saint of Hopeless Causes.

The tar-paper dwellings
and the pulp-log chute
are long gone.
But it's still the same
residential stretch of highway.

I have to pass through there
every time I'm on my way
to almost anywhere.

Every several yards or so
there's a sign
carefully splashed
or painstakingly splattered
in black paint
on a piece of picket fence
broken board
or crooked plywood.

The signs read
Worms For Sale.

Because I'm so uncertain
of my destination
whenever I'm passing through there
I find myself reading
all the Worms For Sale signs.

One by one
they remind me where I'm going.

And that's
when I hear me saying
to myself
to the citizens of The Chute
to my mother
to her friends
and to mine:

P.S. Say me to St. Jude.

♦♦♦

Charmer
(for Lorna Crozier)

We are gathered at our house
in Corner Brook, Newfoundland.

A couple of rooms
full of writers and people.

One of the writers is Patrick Lane.
One of the people is my mother.

She is going on seventy.
He is passing through puberty.

They haven't met yet.
So I introduce them.

"Mom, this is Patrick Lane.
Pat, this is my mother, Mary."

"I'm pleased to meet you, Patrick"
says my mother.
"You have beautiful breasts"
says Patrick.

I take a deep breath
and wait for the knife.

My mother can thrust a very keen blade
in the face of a rude remark.

I know she'll not throw a tantrum
or create a scene or anything like that.

But I know she can cut any man or woman
down to size with a razor sharp phrase
and walk away done with it.

I am still holding my breath.
I am waiting.
I am prepared to say
"Mom, don't mind Pat. He's a poet.
He doesn't know any better."

"Why, Patrick" she says, her blue eyes
soft and bright. "What a lovely thing
to say. Thank you."

Thank you?
I am dumbfounded.
Flabbergasted.

When I tried to grow up
in my mother's house
"breast" was a four-letter word.
Bad and forbidden.

"Could I get you another, Mary?"
Patrick asks casually, politely.
"Yes" my mother replies.
"Bacardi and ginger, please."

I need a refill too. Several.

So I leave them there together
and head for the Screech
on the kitchen table.

Many glasses later
I see over shoulders
through the haze of alcohol
and cigarette smoke
Patrick Lane and my mother
somewhere in the vicinity
of the kitchen sink conversing
about God-knows-what. And I think
"Well, I'll be damned!"

And I damn well would have been
had I said anything like that
to anyone's mother.

But then, that was Lane.
That was my mother.
And obviously at the time
I didn't know either of them
all that well.

◆◆◆

What my Father said about Sound

How to describe the sound
of the sea in a way you can
carry in your pocket
or in your head!
That is the problem.
And cannot be solved.
Roar, swish, crash, whisper, splash!
None of these will do.
Nor any other word.

The sounds the sea makes
are the sea's alone.
They do not belong
to poets or musicians.
Or even to fishermen
who live with those sounds
always in their sleep.

Bong may do for a bell.
Squish may do for water
in your shoes. Crack
may do for a skull
when lightning strikes.
But nothing will do
for the noise the sea makes
in any of its many motions.

This is a good thing.
It will keep the poets
and musicians struggling
as long as there are poets
and musicians to struggle.

When, if ever, someone discovers
the right word (or echo of any kind)
then there's an end to poetry
and music and (perhaps)
even sound itself.

♦♦♦

MAIDEN VOYAGE
(for Clyde Rose)

My friend has a new boat.
It is old and weather-beaten.
The fellow who sold it to him for a song
calls it a dory. It bears no resemblance
to a dory. But it is a boat.
It floats.

It is August 4th, Christmas Day
in Bonne Bay.

The sun shines on the water.
Shines on the brand-new old boat.
And on my friend. Today the sun
is inside him, not a cloud in sight.
It is a fine day on the land.
On the water. And inside someone's soul
who is all child and pirate. Landlubber elf.
Sea roving rambler. Wise old toddler, pretending
this is his daughter's boat. His gift to her.

This isn't a lie. It's an innocent excuse
for his jingle-bell joy here by the sea
under the summer sun.

"She could do with a bit of paint," he says.
And describes with what pleasure his daughter
will undertake that cosmetic task in time.

For now there is only the boat as she is, and
the anticipation of her maiden voyage. Creaky
old, leaky old groaning crone of a maiden.
She will ride my friend and his cargo of dreams
downshore to the nearest tavern.
Or all the way to The Azores.

I stand by as he shoves off, ships the oars
and rows away to his destination, his destiny,
which, for the moment, are the same as those
of any middle-aged boy with his very own boat.
They await his arrival somewhere out there, out
of sight, beyond vision, beyond belief, beyond
any grown man's grasp.

From the crest of a wave, his back to the horizon
he waves to me. And I wave back wishing him,
in fabled sea-faring fashion: "Lots of luck.
A good fuck. And a fair wind home."

♦♦♦

Father of the Bride
(for Kyran)

On this your wedding day
I am rushing around
spinning from store to store
trying to find
a pair of slacks that fit.

I'm not short, tall, fat, or thin.
I am extremely average.
And apparently far too typical
for the tailors and retailers
of men's clothing.

With no time to spare,
sweating it out in cupboard-sized cubicles,
fraught with claustrophobia
and a host of other phobic fears,
I am perilously close to panic.

I've been told
I have to give you away.

I'll not give you away
to anyone.

I will,
with a generous heart,
share you with the man you love.

I'll not give you away.
But I do want to be
a respectable presence
at your wedding.

I have less than an hour
and fifteen miles to go.
And finally in a closet
at the Corner Brook Co-op Store
I try on a pair of denim slacks
that almost fit.
I have a shirt, a jacket
and a tie at home.

Now, in the nick of time,
I'm all set.

I know now that I'll not be
a wrinkle, rip or rumple
in your day. I won't be
an irreverent exception to the rule
in the well dressed, well pressed,
gracefully groomed flow
of your cortege.

I know now I can appear to be
compatible, disappear in the crowd.

I know now
(if only I can get there on time)
that you will forgive me my attire
as I proceed with speed
and all my love
to walk down that aisle with you,
my dear and darling daughter,
to do what I have to do -

to give you away.

◆◆◆

The Cat in the Snow

After all this time (after the divorce
and all that) I come upon the woman
who was my wife for twenty-five years
of my adolescent life.

It is midnight in winter.
Walking alone, for the sake
of walking alone, I come upon her
crouched in ridiculous posture
whispering incoherent pleas
to a snowbank.

"What in God's name are you doing?"
I ask.

"There's a cat" she says.
"It's been roaming around all evening."

She has sought it out
to offer it shelter for the night.
She's been following and coaxing
the lost and lonely feline for an hour now.

But the cat doesn't trust her.
It doesn't know her. Doesn't know
her kindness to strangers, stragglers,
waifs, orphans, stray animals, or any kind
of human kind.

Her house (her home) emptied of me,
is now a sanctuary,
a heart-warming haven for whatever
and whoever is lost, homeless, and left alone.

While I am thinking this, the cat comes creeping
over the snowbank. Cautiously it inches its way
down the iridescent incline
toward my once-upon-a-lifetime lover.
She and the cat are purring cat language
to each other. And now the animal is in her arms.
The rescue accomplished she turns toward home.
"The poor creature!" she says. And then
"Goodnight Al."

I say "I hope you find it a good home."

"I hope you find one too," she says.

Without a word I wish them both a good night
and go my way (way past midnight)
into the empty and endless winter dark.

◆◆◆

The Voices Downstairs

You may tell yourself
those aren't voices you hear
downstairs, that they are simply
the noises houses make at night.
But you aren't convinced.
You listen. And you hear voices.
Familiar voices. And you can almost
make out what they are saying.
At least you can tell they
aren't the voices of burglars
or unwelcome guests. They are
sitting at the kitchen table.
Perhaps they are drinking wine
or coffee or beer. Now and then
you hear a word or two distinctly.
One, a woman, speaks your name.
You lie still and listen. Until
you decide you aren't dreaming
or hearing things. Then you get
logical. A few of your friends
have dropped in. The lights
out, the door unlocked, it
hasn't occurred to them you'd be
in bed this time of night. They
are waiting for you to arrive home.
You decide to get up and join them.
You tell yourself this is good.
You could do with some company.
Glad for this gentle intervention
in the night you tramp lightly
downstairs. Only to discover
the kitchen in darkness. Empty.

Just as you'd left it. There are
no people. There were no voices.
You knew that all along, of course.
And yet as you stumble wide-eyed
back to bed, you wonder who
the woman was. And what it was
she was saying to her phantom friends
while mentioning incidentally, and
so softly, your name.

◆◆◆

The Woman in the Waterfront Bar

Framed in the open doorway
the sun is setting into the red sea.
You come in like a crimson wave.
The sun dies in your hair.

Our eyes burn in their sockets
at the sudden sight of you, the sheer
flow of your entrance. As quick as sin
we strip you naked in your stride.

Like a bright tide rising you sway
through these tables thronged
with drunk sea men and their most
unbeautiful women.

You leave desire drowning in your wake
like bagged cats. Our hands claw
at glasses, bottles, cigarette packs,
pockets. We have decided to hate you.

As you sit now stark stockinged
one tight leg thigh-high over the other
as smooth as wax, we of the cold seas
loathe you with a passion as thick as ice.

We were well sheltered here until you
swept in surfacing the damned debris
of our shipwrecked wishes, the drowned
dreams of our long-lost lives.

Now you have us moaning like mourners
at the casket you carry concealed
between you thighs. Our ice-aged manhood
melts and drips with every drop we drink.

My wild friend, Walt the Whaler, spy-glasses
you with his only eye and whispers Ahoy!
Humpbacks and mermaids are all he's ever loved.
Now he is weeping in his whiskers.

Billy, the bosun, one hand navigating the scar
along his cheek, the other overflowing with
a fist full of fat knee flesh beneath the table,
imagines himself smothering in blubber.

He goes for his knife. The blade turns
to rubber in his grip. He swills and swears.
I sit starboard of the rest and stare
deep into the whisky in my glass.

I am caught in a collision of icebergs.
The ocean is amber. I am drowning.
I will not cry out to you. I will go down
suffering my cowardice with courage.

If you crippled a little in your walk,
if your mouth held some indelible twitch,
if the light from the bar did not adorn you
so, if you sat less perfectly poised,

I would summon up whatever store of grace
I've abandoned to the high seas and come
to you stiff-blooded and brave. I'd pirate
you away in the moon slick night.

I'd sail in your arms, hull down
in the soft swell of your breasts.
I'd anchor my passion in the harbour
of your sighs. And all the seven seas

Would sing their windy songs in praise
of our leeward love. But there is no warp
in your long-legged walk, no twist
in your oh-so-easy smile, no such imperfection

To inspire my courage or my hope.
Tonight you will lie down in Heaven
knows whose arms and wherever I lie
you will be by me, a loving absence

In my embrace. And I'll not sleep, not
succumb, until I have exhausted you
from my want. Come morning you will be
long gone. You will not have mattered

At all. We will store our gear and get
underway for the Greenland sea. There will
be no farewell, no longing left behind, no
harpoon pain in the heart. No death.

Oceans from now, walking the dark decks
under the cold stars, we will forgive you
this distress. Tonight only, we wish you
a bed of kelp, serpents at your flesh

And a quick decay like ours.

❖❖❖

The Dandelion Killers
(for John Steffler)

They hate yellow blossoms
and stems whose winged seeds
can clock a lover's fate.

They prefer one shade
and shape of green, grave high,
as level as death.

They crouch in their houses
like soldiers at siege.
Stockpiled in the basement,
a lethal array of weapons.
All their purpose to kill
the colour yellow.

They dwell in panic
and must ever be alert.
The yellow enemy might return,
invade the lawn, thrive again,
spread into the kitchen,
the living room, the bedroom.
The bed.

Imagine having to make love
in a bed full of dandelions.
One hand on your lover's breast,
the other around the throat
of a flower. And not knowing,
night after night, which of you
will be first to touch the agony
of the other's golden death.

◆ ◆ ◆

The Agony in the Garden
(for David Freeman)

The whole harvest of her lifelong labour
is one tomato, green as emerald,
hard as marble, gleaming in the rain.

She surveys it daily. Morning,
noon, and just before dusk, lifts it
gently, measures the stability
of its fragile grip on the vine,
the tensile strength of the stem.

Should she take it now?
Sever the umbilical cord?
Incubate it to ripeness
on the indoor window sill?

Or give it another day of green growth
among the limp, wilted, still-born stalks,
doomed to decay where she planted,
with such care, her hopes of a small,
but bountiful harvest?

All her lovelorn longing is focused now
on this obstinate green globe,
around which she cradles her hand
as delicately as one would hold
the head of a new-born child.

All she asks in return
for her earth-bound labour
is a full term delivery. The fruit
half-grown enough to have suckled

the last of its nutrition
from the gravel and the ever-absent sun.
Its own gentle welcome into the hollow
of her hand, the hollow of her heart.

To come indoors to be nursed
into ripeness, red as blood.
To be sanctified on the window sill.
While, in the garden, the grubs grab,
cluster and gloat like locusts
swarming within the pages of The Bible.
This is the legacy of her life,
her own new testament to the dreams
she held and dreaded within her womb.

One stubborn tomato
struggling, striving to survive.

All summer long she has come devoted
to her graveyard garden, knelt
devoutly in prayer at her vegetable shrine.
Her morning, noon, and evening angelus
has sustained whatever hope she's held
all this way to the day of harvest.

There it is on the window sill.
A tomato turning from yellow
to red, to rot. An old woman watching it
like a clock winding down to death.

Perhaps it was that Gethsemene
was just another garden.

And this one of them was hers.

❖❖❖

Ashes, Ashes! All Fall Down
(for Gerry Squires)

The flames
that almost
burnt out my daughters
did burn down
your painted portrait of me.

The layers of paint
the glass
the metal frame
all consumed
gone to ash.

All those years
before the fire
Rasputin-like
(all hair and whiskers
and unblinking sockets)
I kept a critical eye
on myself from a secure vantage
where I hung
head and shoulders
above everyone else
who ever sat
in my living room.

Some who sat there
weren't all that fond
of your rendition.

"You look evil!" someone said.
And someone else said

"But we know you aren't."
Perhaps I was.
And perhaps I am.
Maybe all this fumbling and bumbling
is unforgivable
and has been dangerous
to those I have loved without malice
embraced without courage.

"What evil lurks in the hearts of men?"

God only knows!

And who could have known
when I was a child
how mistaken I was
to have imagined
that the living room
was the only room in the house
you might never die in?

I used to wonder then
if all the other rooms
upstairs and downstairs
were dying rooms.

And could you possibly die
while living in the living room?

Years past most
of what mattered then
your portrait of me
presided harmlessly
over all.

Until the afternoon of the fire.
My daughters escaped
from the dying rooms
just in time
to be excited
about not being dead
while I went up
in flames
in the living room.
No more to reign
over my own reign of terror.
All my evil gone to ashes.
The only good looks
I've ever had
gone to dust.

Now as I lie here
in this brand new living room
with walls as barren and bare
as any naked space
I've ever known
I lie here
dying of death
hoping for some portrait
of Jesse James
or Jesus Christ
(any good-hearted hero)
to emerge out of the shadows
to take my place
where I once dangled
like an icon of evil
a third person
hanging heavily
around my neck.

Your portrait of me
died in the living room
in a blaze without glory.

My daughters are alive.
And lovely.

If there's ever a next time
do me a favour.
Paint me cosmetic.
Good. And brave.
Like someone
you could come to
seeking help.
Someone who'd be willing
to die for you
or anyone else
who came to my living room
seeking refuge
from the lives they live
in the living rooms
they are scared to death
of dying in.

❖ ❖ ❖

Prayer
(for Smokey in Hospital)

Once I had a guardian angel
and I used to write notes to him.
He was a him. I was certain of that then.
And I used to write
"Dear Guardian Angel." And the first word
after that salutation was always "Please."
I remember "Please leave me alone."
He didn't for the longest time.
But in time he got fed up
with my stubborn resistance to virtue
and left me quite alone.
I've often since felt sorry for him, imagining
him with no one's right ear to whisper warnings in.
I imagine him slumped up against
some celestial cloud in Heaven's
unemployment line, reduced to remorse
and cheap elixir. All his ambition gone
to Hell with my good intentions.
He didn't have to fuck off just because
I told him to. It was a bad night
and I was angry at everyone, including myself.
But I hurt his feelings I guess
or he decided he didn't want to spend
the rest of my lifetime being a failure.
So whap, flap! Just like that he took off.
He was a good angel. And I know
he's up there somewhere drooping along
in the dark lanes of Paradise, his wings
barely able to support him; like a drunk
on crutches. But he used to be a good
guarding angel. Tonight I'm on my knees

praying "Please" again. "Please God, send
my guardian angel to my friend. They need
each other. I know he has his own but
just this once you could let someone have
two. Couldn't you? Just in case one of them
gets pissed off and flies away." I think
this time my angel will be the one who stays.
He'll want to. And I believe (now that
he's learned his lesson) he will.

♦♦♦

Kelly at Graveside
(for Rufus Guinchard)

In this wind-blown, wild-flowered
fenced-in meadow by the sea, this
bleak September day, we are the silent,
sombre witnesses to your burial
in the black earth.

The wind off the water is blowing the grass
as flat as a blanket, a green-grown shroud.
We lean into it, knowing this is as close
as we will ever get to you again.

A few feet (immeasurable miles)
north-north-east of your grave
(the hole in the ground you are
being put to bed in), your friend
and fellow fiddler, Kelly Russell,
stands upright in the wind, in stoic reverence.

I don't know what he's feeling.
I know only that he knows
you are going down, forever.

Later in the lounge down the road,
I think of the awful, wonderful burden
of his dual legacy.

His father was to this island with his words
what you have been to us with your music.
A glad burden, no doubt, to carry
beyond the grave. This, and that grave.

His father's words and your music, the language
that defines us, informs this silence, this rush
of wind, all our reasons for being here.
It all thrives alive in Kelly, standing there
at your graveside suffering his own grief,
commemorating his own infant history, as quiet
as a blank page, as silent as a stringless fiddle.

You are going down into the ground.
Close by, north-north-east of your grave, you are
alive and well. You are upright in the wind,
standing still in the gulf-battered grass
with all your music tingling in someone's
heart, his pocketful of fingers.
If there's anything at all to eternity, this is it.

This is how your life goes on.

This is how you live now as we turn away
from this raw wound in the earth, turn to go
down the road with our heart's consignment
of words, music, and everlasting silence.

❖❖❖

The Dance of the Mayflies

We who have known
and yet long for lasting love
cannot ascend to that space
wherein the mayflies
dance their dance and die.

We may lament the brevity
of their agile joy, their consummation
in the shallow altitudes of the air.

We may envy them the choreography
of their airborne ballet, their winged
copulation in the summer sun.

But they aren't odes or rhymes
on wings. They aren't symbols
of beauty or emblems of ecstasy.

They are insects who are born
to dance one dance and die.

Because our destinies
are less defined than theirs
we need to know there'll always be
a morning after and always
another night to stumble, lame
and wingless, into darkness.

Unlike the mayflies (but maybe not)
we need to live on, living in love
beyond the limits of our own
mortality. We have to keep on dying
day after day, night after night.
Dying again and again, over
and over, for the next, only
and always one more dance.

❖❖❖

Limbo Dancer

Because they didn't get to you in time
you missed out on your ticket to Heaven.

The priest's prayers were a waste of words.
The holy water dribbled in vain
down the veins of your unholy head.

They buried you in that portion of ground
reserved for you and your fellow exiles,
those who had been consigned to Limbo
before you.

Now I'd like to know
how you're doing after all those years
out there in eternal nowhere.

Maybe you ought to consider
yourself lucky (your unblemished soul
suspended somewhere in the simple dark
untouched by joy, torment, or remorse
for either) because no state of grace
had ever been bestowed on you.

I suppose I could have been
looking forward to Heaven by now
had I done most things differently.
But as it happens it looks like
I'm going to Hell in a handbasket.

In any case, I'd choose to last
as long as I could here on earth
where love welcomes us
to live in defiance of death.

When I was so much younger
and you would have been much
younger still, there was a dance
going around here: a version
of a dance they did, long before
you and I were born, in a place
they call The Caribbean.
I used to pretend to myself then
that it originated in Limbo
where all the souls
were double-jointed acrobats
(wriggling in rhythm
a fraction of an inch
beneath bamboo barrier sticks
flaming with hell-fire
and held dangerously down
by fallen angels) dancing
their dance to the beat of eternity
and having one heck of a good time
doing it.

That was, of course, a silly twist
of theology. A demented dance of the mind.

Yet, from time to time, I think
of you out there wherever Limbo is.
You fetal feet firm in the solid void,
your new-born body bent flat back
in the black abyss, your frail arms
waving in embryonic rhythm at nothing there
in the endless expanse between Heaven
and Hell.

Tonight, just a short stroll
from your bit of burial ground, I think:
Keep on dancing, my infant
un-named brother in no-one's arms.
Bless us now with your dead desire
to dance on Earth.
Dance 'til the consecrated stars
die in the sky, 'til the lights go out
over all our graves.

Keep on dancing, kid!
Keep on dancing 'til the end of time.

♦♦♦

From
THIRTY FOR
SIXTY
2000

The Pink, White and Green
(for Des Walsh)

The flag flat out.
The grass bent south-south-east.
The man mowing the meadow
is no gardener of gardens.
It just happens to be a good day
to take care of the country.

The waist-high hay falls away
in sea-green sheets with every swipe
of the stone-honed blade he swings
at the leaning field while cursing
this year's crop of resurrected rocks.

Without a wrinkle in the wind
the flag flies high overhead.

The man mowing the meadow
knows exactly who he used to be
when he took care of his land
without a care for anything
in the world outside those
four fortress fences, fading away now
to the colours of corruption and decay.

He knows the fence needs fixing and
the house uphill, a new coat of paint.
The latch on the garden gate ought to be
replaced, the clothesline pole secured.
But for now, today, there's the land
to be looked after, and the wind
is just right to slice the grass down hill
to the end of the overgrown slope
he's cared for always and only because
it was his and his alone. And theirs.

Back on to the house he's well aware
of his widow up there in the window
watching him sweep the summer's growth of grass
down to the ground, low below
the Pink, White and Green flag
flying high above the only nation
he and she have ever known.

❖❖❖

Lupins
(for Frieda)

Across the ditch by the graveyard fence
a groundbound rainbow of purple and pink.

Triumphant yesterday in the Trinity Bay sun.
Courageously upright today
in this day's torrential downpour.

I come upon them suddenly
at a quick twist in the twisted road.
Whatever the weather, they are here
this summer season like a bright ribbon
of light, not quite, but almost
out of sight.

Behind and above them, sleeping deep
in the rainsoaked earth, the dead rest
deep in peace.

Below, the waves wash
in their eternal turn upon
the Goose Cove shore.

Making my way to Trinity
in this morning's morning deluge
(soaked to the skin and bereft of love)
I would tip my hat to the trinity
of the sea, the dear departed
and the lupins blooming between.

I don't happen to have a hat on my head
but I do wear a prayer in my heart.
I make a secret Sign of the Cross
and say silently inside to the one god
who doesn't believe in me, "God bless
the long and just gone dead, the sullen
slate-grey sea, and especially (now)
I pray, please bless the lupins blooming there
upright (purple, pink) and right as rain."

◆◆◆

The Citrus Sea
(for Tana)

Somewhere at sea the oceans shift.
Twenty tons of tropical fruit go overboard.
Tidal waves of lemons floating west.

Wearing only her little laced and latticed
bathing suit, she wobbles to the end of the world.

She's a child. She knows what's real
and what isn't. And now she's about to walk
on water.

Her parents (intent on the intensity
of their efforts to love one another)
are oblivious to the miracle at hand.

Within the seaside, sunlit desperation
of their embrace, they are unaware
that their toddling daughter
is about to alter all they've never known
of themselves and each other.

In the middle of their struggle
for love, she has waded her way
to the edge and end of everything.

The galaxies swirl and curl.
The golden waters beckon.

She trembles in. And goes under.
Comes up splashing in a sea of lemons.
Yellow waves wash over her. She surfaces
for the second time. Goes down for the third.
All this before she knows
what lemons are, what yellow is.

Knowing only what much
there was to know in this world
she has wandered into another
for which she (and they) have no name now.
Nor ever will.

◆◆◆

Lambs to the Slaughter

She told me this twice.

There were lambs prancing
in the pasture. And it was
coming on slaughter time.

She was fond of the cows
(goats, roosters and corn).
But she dearly adored the lambs.

She knew what little and as much
as she could (in her little age) about
life and death on her father's farm.
And even then she knew the lambs
would never grow up to be sheep.
But above all, she wanted to be
there the day they went. It would have been
a time never to be forgotten.

She hadn't seen anything killed except
carrots and cabbages and trees. The only
blood she'd ever seen had been her own
and that of some Sunday supper's hen.

Counting the days (without knowing
what day) she went to sleep each night
reciting the litany of the names
she had named the lambs.

When the day came, she was sent away
to an uncle's acres many miles down
the road to spend the afternoon playing
make-believe with her cousins.

Her father (aware of her love for the lambs)
had decided the death of them ought to be
done in her absence. And when her uncle
ushered her in the door (the afternoon gone)
it was all over. Death was done.

She hasn't since forgiven her father
for having taken that day out of her life.

"I don't hate him," he said.
"I just can't forgive him."

She told me this twice. Once before
and once after. And there, in the sadness
of her sad grip, I wept for her, for her father
and all things (like that night) gone for good
and too close to get back to ever again.

◆◆◆

Standing Room Only

I tell this not as I would in Confession
but without a word of a lie.

At the height of his golden trumpeting
"High Society" career of fame
and fortune, Louis Armstrong waved
his famous cotton kerchief at me
from a bandstand in a hockey rink
in Corner Brook, Newfoundland.

That was the night I declined to go
to Hell for the sake of love then or thereafter.

Danny Barcelona played the drums.
Satchmo played his golden horn
and sang deep down to all the lovers
he'd ever and never known, while
Susan and I danced to the magic
of the music and all things so suddenly possible.

At intermission we went for a ride
in my father's old Oldsmobile. The music
had made the promise of everything
come true. In the old quarry where we
parked, we held on to each other like lovers
on the brink of love until it came
to toss-up time between time and Eternity.

That's when I stammered (stupidly)
"We'd better get back."
Without a word all the way, we returned
to the rink, rigged out for the night like
a nightclub in Monte Carlo or Hollywood.

That's the last I saw of Susan. She (and
whoever he was) danced one dance
after another while I sat forlorn, alone
on a bench in the bleak bleachers
above and beyond the end of the dream
that was never to be anything but.

When I turned away from what I had forsaken
down there on the flood-lit floor, I saw a sign
that read "Standing Room Only."

Danny Barcelona beat out a solo
that would have made Gene Krupa
roll over. Louis Armstrong wiped
his brow with his sweat-wet trademark
and waved it at me where I sat, sad and
solitary, in the empty attic of the night.

I waved my applause back at him.
He lifted his horn and blew one
long lilting note that faded finally
in the dim rafters low overhead.

And that's the note I left on.

Driving my father's Rocket '88
home, I held on to the steering wheel
for dear life and to my immortal soul
for all and what little it was worth.

Louis Armstrong has since died.
Susan has since married. I am
still alive without a hope
in hell of ever going to Heaven.
Remembering that night, I recall lying

wide awake in bed (the car parked
secure, inviolate in the driveway)
and remember God the Father
whispering at me through the metal mesh window
dividing the double dark closets
in which we were confined as though
we were locked together in Limbo.

I confessed my temptation without a fib.
Father So-and-so said "Ego te absolvo."
And then, "For your penance say three Hail Marys."

The absolution granted, the penance
prescribed, there in the dark of that dismal
dungeon, I was blessed and dismissed
to an eternity of celibate sainthood.

I've prayed a lot of prayers since then.
And spent a lot of time kneeling on my knees.

But also since, I've promised myself, Satchmo
(and all the saints who've gone marching in)
that long before the last blast of the trumpet
sounds, I'll be among the lowest of the low-down
dancers below here and hereafter.

And that's a promise I promise to keep
until my knees give out or the music stops.
Having spent so much time in a state
of grace, Heaven hardly seems worth the effort.

Therefore I have resolved to "Go and sin
no more." And almost haven't.

◆◆◆

Hard Times

In the middle of a dream
he rolled out of bed
and died that night
stabbed to death
by a bottle he'd broken
in his fatal fall
to the flop-house floor.

There in a dump
called "The American Hotel"
in New York City
he left his blood
for some weary maid
to clean up after him.

There in the crimson smear
at the end of a dream, far, far
from The Swanee River. Far
from the magnolia blooming south
of his songs, Stephen Foster
came to no good end.

There, between destitution and death
his hard times dissolved in darkness.
Then and thereafter they could come
again no more.

Too long had they lingered
around that dead-end door.

"Hard times, hard times come again no more."

❖❖❖

Another Night in Crawley's Cove

The accordion considers the tunes it knows best.
The conversation, though incoherent, is congenial.

Outside, the balsams are dancing in the wind.
(The branches, an orchestra of castanets.)
Somewhere in the sky, the birds are sound asleep.

The giddy dancers are stepping it out
on the floorboards of their spindrift dreams.

Tomorrow, the music will be still, the sky quiet
and the birds will be back in the backyard woods.

The day will pass without measure until
night falls and time begins again. The birds
will take to the sky, the dreamers to their feet
and the floor will endure or enjoy another night
of jigs, reels, knee-slapping yarns, out-of-tune
tunes and foot-stomping songs.

Elsewhere in the cove there are people asleep.
They'll be up and about before dawn, long before
the last lie has been told and we've all gone
to rest in peace.

The old Waterford wood stove has grown cold.
But there's no discomfort here in this elderly house
on the hill. We are contentedly tired and ready
to creep or crawl to our makeshift beds to await
this day's dawning.

The water, lapping at the landwash, will lull us
to sleep until the birds in the balsams wake us
to another day in Crawley's Cove and another night
close to the floor, well removed from the lives
we live when here is far away. And we are elsewhere.

Where we are the most we have of ourselves.
And the least we have of each other.

♦♦♦

The Sea Breeze Lounge

It's a warm overcast Bonne Bay afternoon.
There's a slight north-east breeze on the water.
Inside, Black Hat George is tending bar.
He, myself, and one other patron are the only
people here. The younger man has made his way
to the gambling machine with the aid of some
awkward machinery designed to keep him
upright. A truck ran over him in Toronto
and he's come home to learn to walk again.

The pool table stands staunch on its crutches.
The juke box is silent, all its hurtin' songs
sung to silence because pain can be fatal
and machines and people do break down.

Of course, I'm here too, about to give up
and perhaps give out for good. But for now
I'm one of three survivors who've almost
survived so far. Almost isn't a good feeling
but it shall have to do for now. You are
(my dearest darling, wherever you are)
surviving like the rest of us. I would like
to be of some assistance but the hazards
that have brought me here drag me down
like a heavy harness, an iron cross.

There's not much comfort but plenty
of solitude in The Sea Breeze this overcast
afternoon. There's a determined young man
learning to walk again. There's George
who wears his black hat with wild-west
authority. He has one leg left and a vigorous
hop in every step he takes down the seaside

street at high noon, sunset or any time of day.
And there's me, the picture of health
and wholeness (scared to death to stand up
lest I fall flat on my face).

I think it's worth it, whatever else our obstinate
ailments are, that we don't fall down, that all three
of us (and you) do our best to walk upright
and go with hope to wherever we are bound.

Right now I know we three could use a drink.
And this round's on me. But, most of all as far
from here as you happen to be this round's
a toast to you, your agility and your vigorous ascent
to the top of your dreams.

◆◆◆

The Fuller Brush Man

Behind the bar
your day's work done
you've just released your hair
from its rhinestone shackle.

Now it shines in these shadows
like moonlight on water
(starshine in the darkest night)
and when you move it shimmers
from your waist up like a veil
of sequins, diamonds or gold dust.

From here where I sit remembering
I see some several strands gone astray.

And now (only) I permit myself
to imagine my fingers imagining
themselves deliberately and delicately
brushing each wayward wisp
of your hair back into place
(as they take all the time in the world
never getting to the end of anything).

I am remembering once upon a time
when my father was the Fuller Brush man.
His hands brushed my mother's hair
to beauty beyond his own belief
(until his hands died in her hair).
Broke and broken hearted
he left my mother nothing
but the legacy of his marvelous love.

Had you been born when I knew him
he would have welcomed your hair
into his hands as I would (now)
reach out of reach for all things lovely.

And now I learn you haven't been working
behind the bar all day. You've just come
from your father's funeral.

Your encounter with death today
was fuller than that my skeletal hands
would have woven in your hair
for the sake of selling myself
another brush with death –
the guaranteed going of all things
as beautiful as my mother's hair
as passionate as my father's hands –
moonlight on water
(starshine in the darkest night).

♦♦♦

Thirty-for-Sixty

My father was a man of metaphors.
When he said to me, "Don't wait
until you have the five in your hand
before you go thirty-for-sixty"
He wasn't talking about cards.

Newfoundland's national pastime
is a game of Growl (otherwise called
Auction or A Hundred and Twenties).
Thirty-for-sixty is the ultimate bid.
To make that bid without the five
of trumps in your hand is a foolish
thing to do. Chances are (nine times
out of ten) you'll end up in the hole.

So what! When it's just a game.
A bit of fun. What the hell!

But that night as he lay dying
he wasn't talking about cards.
No overdose of morphine
could diminish his need to leave
his son one last word of wisdom.

I listened and took him to heart.

I've been going thirty-for-sixty
without the five ever since.

The hole grows deeper and deeper.

And now it's my turn to bid again.
I don't have the five in my hand
and I've little else to go on.

But what the hell!

Thirty-for-sixty!

♦♦♦

A River Runs Through Her

Coming on dark, the loons lament
the slow closing of the sky. And she's
out there having one more flick.

The rod, the reel, the line
are extensions of her self.

Here (hidden in twilight)
I watch from the river bank
and wonder what some stranger
might think if she were his mother
out there in that current
going for the legal limit
at age eighty-three.

Would he stand here in the shelter
of these trees where I stand safe
on shore shielding myself from the realities
that surround me, and think "That's my mother.
She's the flow my father swam in?"

The last cast. The feathered fly afloat.
The sudden splash. The leap of the heart.
The frantic landing.

She rows ashore in the dawn of dark.

I leave the trees, the loons and the river
and slip away in the sudden comfort
of darkness.

I am the stranger.
Though she is my mother
I know nothing of this woman.
I know only that a river runs through her.

And I splash in her blood like a fish.

◆◆◆

A Bouquet for Emily

These frail flowers will not last
the length of your journey.
They'll not stay in bloom long enough
to decorate your destination
or bless your destiny with blossoms.

They are buttercups given only
to lament the gladness of your going.

As you always have, you will go
on tip-toe, summer-saulting
and cart-wheeling all the way.

These fragile flowers will wilt
long before this beginning begins.

But whatever awaits you (wherever
you go) won't matter as long
as what fate rains down on you
is as golden as these petals are now
and as you have been in all seasons
beneath the meadows in the sky
lighting the fields with love and laughter
upsidedown and homeward bound
ever brighter than the brightest light.

I shall be forever fond of those fields
and the flowers blooming there wild
(with you within) as I walk among them
bending the long grass in the shadow
of your green and golden glow.

Because there's little else to offer
(now as you depart) I pass you
this fistful of flowers, wish you
heaps and leaps of love, lots of luck
and quiet smiles all the way home.
Always with buttercups growing
from the ground up and the sky down.

◆◆◆

The Annunciation

You, my lovely daughter (your
immaculately conceived conception
concealed by all but the bulge
of your belly, curtained
by your blessed flesh, hidden
from the world about to be born
into the world-wide warmth
of your embrace) are here now
on the eve of everything
this while before the world turns
and there is no returning.

Somewhere along the way
we've all been born. And always
there've been mothers and fathers
and the umbilical beginning
of all things future, holy and profane.

Your child is yours now only
for this tiniest of times. Soon
the tidal-wave world will spill in
and this wonder will ebb
as your wishes wash, spread
and splash over cradle and crib
and the world's turning tide
outruns your child's first footsteps
up the kelp-covered landwash
to the wind-bent meadow
where little mice hunt, hide and seek
and there is life and sudden death
then, there and ever thereafter.
There'll be photographs of your father.
Stories to tell. Yarns to spin.
And songs to sing. All barely credible
and none of them true. Except you.

You shall be the truth of me alive
as once I was when my father lived
never to live happily ever after in love
with grass, trees, snow, all things in bloom
and children outdoors in all seasons.

Then, the yard and the woods around
overflowed with birds and animals.
Swarms of insects, rain, hail, snow
and sunshine and bats by the billions
filled the air and the swift swallows
swooped over the river that flowed
ever west where the heavens bent
gently to genuflect below the slow, low
hanging clouds on the high horizon.

There, on the edge of eternity
by the eternal river, we'd lie silent
on the slant, sand-banked beach
and peer deep down into the dark
and bottomless starlit sky.

Now, there's this new and other
high horizon for you, your child and us
(all your long-lost and everlasting lovers).

But look! In the dark and starless sky
this north November night, the sun
is rising here where your sanctity shines
within and shall shine for as long as
infinity lasts and forever is.

For "Blessed is the fruit of thy womb."
And thee.

◆◆◆

To Kyran in Full Flight

The borders you must cross to get to Mexico
are nothing compared to the borders
you've crossed to get to where you are.

Going toward yourself is
the longest journey of all.

There are instruments to help you
get to San Miguel de Allende.
But the southbound bird winging
its way south without map or compass
holds within its heart some knowing
unknown even to itself.

Your lover awaits your arrival
in full knowledge that you have been
his destiny all along. The artist
who painted your portrait portrayed you
as a bird imprisoned on its perch.
Your expression there—
the grim anticipation of flight.

Now (fold upon fold of that feathered grip let go)
you've taken to wing. Now you have no instruments
to guide you. And now your destination
has nothing to do with Mexico.

The horizons tumble away as they leap-frog
forever forward in front of you. Your journey
is the journey that has no end.

I will miss you. And I will envy your lover
his destiny under the ancient Aztec sun.
But as long as you travel the endless skyways
to (and ever toward) your heart's delight
I'll be there with you, soaring somewhere
alongside—winging it all the way.

❖❖❖

Homecoming
(for Alden)

You are too lately born
to know where you are.

Arkansas! Newfoundland!
What's the difference but for
the immediacy of the floor
beneath your face, the familiar
comfort of the foreign bed
you share, always aware
of what's within your ever groping grasp?

One day you'll know all you'll want
to know about Newfoundland. And
maybe, some other day, you'll return.
Your Arkansas friends may ask
"Where y'all going?"

"Newfoundland," you'll reply
as though it were somewhere
just up there in The Ozarks.

"Where's that?"

"It's an island in the sky
just north of the Northern Star
and it's full of fairies, ghosts
and goblins. It's as old as the stars
(as cold as ice) and warm as embers."

"When will you be back?"

"Sometime! Soon! But I gotta go now
and ask my mom if she'll wrap and roll
my carpet. I'm off to Newfoundland
first thing in the morning."

"See ya!"

"See y'all, soon."
Then you'll take off and land nowhere
on Earth and feel whatever you feel
at home on a starlit beach dancing
with the fairies, the ghosts and goblins
by the slap-happy sea as the Blomidon Mountains
dive deep down to the water's waltzing edge
and The Northern Lights sing in the sky
to welcome you, as we do now and will
whenever you return here to here.

To the fairies, the ghosts, the goblins. And to us.

◆◆◆

Rites of Passage
(for Janice and Gerard)

Whatever little time we live, time
in the end, adds up to no time at all.
Sadly and gladly there are things
to be seen in the sun and missed
in flight along the way.

We take to wing, fly a while, ponder
all that circles below us and descend
to earth. We look up to see where
we've been. We measure the spaces
we inhabit inside, out and about.

The ground beneath our feet
is our foothold for as long as we
can stand and hang on. The sky
is where birds and angels dwell.
We've all been visitors there and come
back home to the back yards of Heaven.

The sky is where we've been when
we've gone to sleep undreaming
or been wide awake, night and day
alert to our own mortality.

But however low below the slow clouds
we strive to thrive, the sun burns above.

And keeps on burning.

◆◆◆

www.ingramcontent.com/pod-product-compliance
Lightning Source LLC
Chambersburg PA
CBHW071712090426
42738CB00009B/1746